Walking with God: Repairing the Breach and Restoring the Ancient Path of Discipleship

Wayland Henderson

Walking with God:

Repairing the Breach and Restoring the Ancient Path of Discipleship

Wayland Henderson

Dedications

I dedicate this book to my beautiful and wonderful wife Jeanette for always encouraging me to pursue God with radical abandonment. To my wonderful children Jaleesa, Michael, and Moriyah. You all will always be my first and most important ministry.

Thank you to my editor Dr. Brenda Boerger for your expertise and heart for the Father.

Finally this book is dedicated to all the Fathering leaders that I have walked with and the sons and daughters that are walking with me. These pages are the unfolding of the journey we have taken together.

Endorsements

There is a cry in the Spirit right now for the people of God to return to their first love. This book by Wayland Henderson gives voice to that call of the Spirit. In these pages, you will be drawn into the intricate threads of God's complex tapestry, both through teaching and prophetic vision the author gives clarity to the ancient path of a walk with God. Wayland writes as to transfer his own walk into the pages he has written so that you almost feel the dust of the road he has travelled as you read. I believe that contained within this book is not only the information to begin a walk with God, the understanding to discover the deep wells along the path, but also the impartation to carry the passion for restoration and revival carried by the author. This is your invitation to a walk with God that you never imagined, a life of pilgrimage with the King. "Blessed is the man whose strength is in You, whose heart is set on pilgrimage" (Ps. 84: 5). It is time to arise and walk!

Sean D. Harvey, author of Formed in Secret
and Culture of Sonship

As in the days of John the Baptist there was a prophetic message sent forth to make way for the coming of the King and His Kingdom. As he was a forerunning voice and burning and shining lamp that preceded a Kairos moment, and it will be again with a collective kingdom voice that will usher in the greater witness of His Glory to cover the Earth! There is indeed an awakening in the church as Wayland so clearly articulates that is bringing a new and ancient day back to the Body of Christ. It is a return to the ancient path as Jeremiah declared in the OT: Thus says the LORD, "Stand by the ways and see and ask for the ancient paths, Where the good way is, and walk in it; And you will find rest for your souls. But they said, 'We will not walk in it.'

In a time when everyone is looking for answers, many are being brought back to the divine path of discipleship as truth hangs in the balance of our yes. What will you choose and where will you stand while the greatest hour and field of play unfolds? There can simply be no greater joy of moving forward in His light and order as one era comes to a close and gives birth to a fresh blueprint from the mountain into the hands of the local church. As Moses looked and surveyed for a city whose builder and maker was God such there is a generation rising in the earth that is finding the Way of Walking with God and its making room for a proceeding voice with larger than life impact at stake. It is high time to awake so the eyes of the Lord can route many into a spirit of reformation where Sons work the works of God from their kingdom position as they rule and reign from the high seat and vantage point of intimacy.

As a previous era's light and prophetic ministry comes to a close there is a brighter witness and invitation being given to a new and emerging prophetic generation. Wayland so genuinely instructs us to hear and heed the call into the very plumb line of His Heart in this book. There is a pioneering company coming forth in the earth that will build in accordance to the pattern that can only be built by the Inward Christ as they have stood in the counsel of the Lord and seen the Way of Walking with God. This is a rich book that I will be encouraging everyone I know to read. I have never read one like it for it is genuine and unique to Wayland and what he carries.

Tom Ledbetter Founder of Kingdom Gravity Ministries & School of Dream Intelligence, Founder and Elder of Eastgate Community Church".

In the building process of our lives in Christ Jesus, the proper stones must be laid. We gain understanding on how we fit into the cornerstone of Kingdom life's fulfillment upon these stones. One of the key stones is discipleship. I believe Wayland expounds upon that stone within these very pages. The defining steps of discipleship speak to us consistently throughout this book. The purpose and the understanding of key discipleship fundamentals are clearly defined. The path pointed out to us reveals a finishing work of the Holy Spirit who assists as we embark on a new journey. The keys in this book will unlock directives on humility and servanthood within you. As you walk through the pages, ask yourself questions. As you do, the text will unlock specific answers needed for you. This will be a book you will refer to and read over again and again. The heart of true discipleship leads us through the veil of intimacy and prayer and it is a common thread that will invite the reader to enter in as they seek out the purposes of their life's destiny.

Phyllis Ford Cleansing Waters International

Table of Contents

xi

Foreword

To talk about something is not the same as experiencing it. To experience Truth is to be freed from what is not Truth. To experience what you are describing is to become what you are communicating. The truth about the Truth is not the Truth that sets you free.

Much discussion of discipleship does not make disciples. Discipling transforms those that follow their assigned leaders. Modern discipleship indoctrinates people in the truth about the Truth but leaves them completely unaware of the kingdom of God.

Jesus designed discipling to produce a lifestyle that expresses the internal changes redemption and restoration bring to someone following his assigned leader as a means of more fully follow Jesus.

"This is the essence of discipleship...teaching the kingdom so ekklesia can happen," Wayland Henderson says. Wow! This guy gets it!

That statement is worth the entire book. However, this author does more than makes a statement. He "walks" us through this Truth from the beginning to the end, putting it into the context of Biblical history. Before we realize it, he convinces us in a way that makes us bold. We want to experience the fullness of it.

We are entering the most significant decade of history since Jesus walked on Earth. Wayland is calling us to live up to the challenge, to reinstate Bible norms, to establish kingdom culture, to live the life, to be the people of God in the time God offers fathering nations more significant opportunity to transform.

Wayland Henderson backs up his claims, gives them authority, and speaks from experience - he is putting this stuff into practice, not touting theories.

As I read this book, I stopped and thanked God for the treasure the kingdom of God enjoys in mercy. God has not left us without voices and champions of Truth! Wayland offers us the language for God's authentic and original design and definition of kingdom ekklesia.

This is not a "read-it-once-and-put-it-on-a-shelf" book. This book is a workbook, a study guide, and discipling schematic. This volume is a brand-new classic.

If you ever entertained the idea that God would leave us without a radical Remnant, forget it! Wayland Henderson represents the bold hope of a here and now move of God in America and the nations! This book will help solidify that hope with practical vision.

Dr. Don Lynch Author & Founder of MinistryMatrix and Freedom Ministry International

Walking with God:

Repairing the Breach and Restoring the Ancient Path of Discipleship

Chapter 1:
Repairing the Breach and Restoring the Ancient Path

And your ancient ruins shall be rebuilt; you shall raise up the foundations of many generations; you shall be called the repairer of the breach, the restorer of streets to dwell in.
Isaiah 58:12

We have entered into the beginning of a new era and currently stand in the midst of renewal and restoration of both the role and function of the body of Christ, His church here on earth. Prophetically speaking, the Lord has shown me that 2010 to 2020 is a prophetic window where the Spirit of God would cleanse the eyes of His Bride to see clearly, because 2020 would be the beginning of renewed foundations that would radically change how we presently operate as the church. It will be a season of revival and restoration in preparation for reformation. The Father will drop the plumb line to realign us back with the Headship of Christ to be His governmental and legislative extension in the earth. The hearts of the fathers and children are being turned back to each other as the Spirit and power of Elijah increasingly moves to prepare the ancient path of the kingdom.

To accomplish this, the ancient path and restoration of discipleship on an intimate and corporate level must first be restored, so we can walk in the reality of what it means to be a co-heir with Christ as sons of God. Pioneers and forerunners are emerging as repairers of the breach and restorers of ancient paths, in preparation for the coming great harvest. From the Garden of Eden, where Adam walked with God in the cool of the day, until the Book of Revelations, where the Tabernacle or dwelling place of God will fully become man, we are invited to walk with God on a daily basis, learning how to be like Him in our everyday life.

The Disciple, Student, and Scholar

The concept of discipleship is expressed in a profound way in the Book of Isaiah:

> 11 For the Lord spoke thus to me with his strong hand upon me, and warned me not to walk in the way of this people, saying: 12 "Do not call conspiracy all that this people calls conspiracy, and do not fear what they fear, nor be in dread. 13 But the Lord of hosts, him you shall honor as holy. Let him be your fear and let him be your dread. 14 And he will become a sanctuary and a stone of offense and a rock of

2

stumbling to both houses of Israel, a trap and a snare to the inhabitants of Jerusalem. 15 And many shall stumble on it. They shall fall and be broken; they shall be snared and taken." 16 Bind up the testimony; seal the teaching among my disciples.

Isaiah 8:11-16

The Lord *instructs* Isaiah to not walk in the ways of foreign nations or make alliances with them. The word *instruct* is the word *yasar* that means, 'To chasten, discipline, instruct and correct.' *Yasar* derives from the root that means, 'To rule and turn the head and direction of a child or student into a particular direction.'[1] Upon completing the prophecy, Isaiah closes the scroll and according to most Jewish commentators, he gave it to his disciples. The word for *disciple* in Hebrew is *limmud* which means, 'learned, and taught, one who is student or a scholar.' It derives from the root 'to learn by goading or directing the path of the ox by goading it; learning by goading.' The goad is a pointed staff used for directing oxen in a yoke. That is, the principle of discipleship is based on this kind of yoke-goading. That is, prompting a disciple, who has become a student of the word, in a way which leads them towards maturity and responsibility. It is interesting to note that when Saul encounters Jesus on the Damascus Road, Jesus asks Saul, "Why do you kick against the goad?". Discipleship not only refers to teaching, but it is the binding factor of the teacher and disciple in covenantal relationship. The yoke of true discipleship with Jesus is the yoke that will lead us into covenant, into the fullness of our inheritance.

---

[1] Ancient Hebrew Lexicon Bible.
https://www.biblestudytools.com/lexicons/hebrew/

I believe the Spirit of God is inviting us into a realm of intimacy where we can not only fully comprehend what our inheritance involves, but also partner and co-labor with Christ to see the extension of the kingdom of heaven on earth. This book takes you on a journey to see into the heart of Jesus, as you discover what it means to become His disciple and how every area of our lives is impacted by this truth. It is in our everyday walk that the Father desires to train and mature us to be His image-bearers on earth, releasing the greater works of His Son as we co-labor with Him.

Chapter 2
Walking with God

Walking and His Divine Presence

One of my greatest joys in life is being a father to three wonderful children. Raising children, being responsible for their well-being, and having the significant charge to shape their character is a good illustration of what it means to walk with God. My son, ever since he could walk and talk, has always wanted to be like me. Wherever I would go, he wanted to go and whatever I would do, he would try to imitate me to the best of his ability. That is why I gave him the nickname "mini-me". Walking with God carries some of these same principles, where we just want to be like our heavenly Father. The biblical concept of *walking* denotes not just a physical sense of following someone around, but also portrays a lifestyle.

One of the first places the word *walk* is used is Genesis 3:8, where Scripture declares that the voice of the Lord God was *walking* in the cool of the day and Adam became so afraid that he and his wife hid themselves from the presence of the Lord. One of the first principles we see in this text is that *walking* denotes the presence of someone, in this case, the Presence of the Yahweh. From this, we can conclude that *walking with God* is a concept which involves communion and relationship. In the example with my natural son, not only did he follow me around in a literal sense, but also we *walked* together or simply put, we did life together.

In Genesis 3, Scripture declares that Adam heard the sound or voice of the Lord walking in the cool of the day. Because of their disobedience, he and Eve hid themselves from the Presence of the Lord because of their fear of punishment; but it does not say they were surprised. This would indicate that it was not the first time God showed up. In other words. Up until that time Yahweh was doing life with Adam and Eve by continual communion with them. Dr. Michael Heiser, a Semitic and Biblical Scholar, describes it in this fashion:

> "The description of Yahweh 'walking' is also used of God's active Presence inside Israel's tabernacle, creating another link between Eden, the cosmic mountain, and Israel's tabernacle"[2].

The concept of God walking amongst His people denotes his constant dwelling with and among the Israelites.

One of the Biblical prerequisites for being God's spokesperson is that one first had to meet Him in order to be able to speak for Him[3]. Two of the most notable figures in the Old Testament who *walked with God* were Enoch and Noah. Both were representatives and mouthpieces for Yahweh, but neither of them were commissioned through a one-time meeting with God. Rather, *walking* indicates they had a lifestyle of doing life with Yahweh.

Enoch Walked with God

---

[2] Heiser, Michael S. *The Unseen Realm: Recovering the Supernatural Worldview of the Bible.* Bellingham, Washington: Lexham Press, 2015.
[3] Ibid.

Though the Scriptures are limited with regard to the depths of the life and ministry of Enoch, there is adequate context that through the spirit of revelation and the understanding of historical context, we are able to see a powerful truth which is unveiled in the lives of Enoch and Noah.

22 Enoch walked with God after he fathered Methuselah 300 years and had other sons and daughters. 23 Thus all the days of Enoch were 365 years. 24 Enoch walked with God, and he was not, for God took him.

Genesis 5:22-24

These are the only Old Testament Scriptures that describe the life of Enoch; yet they are filled with rich treasure. Scripture affirms that Enoch had never seen death as he encountered God. For Enoch to walk with God for 300 years, he first had to *meet God.*

I believe Enoch is a prophetic picture of what it means for sons to walk in intimate relationship with the Father and learn to reflect His image. According to Scripture, Enoch began to walk with God after he begat Methuselah at the age of 65, and then walked with God for another 300 years. This demonstrates that before Enoch was taken he experienced doing life with the Creator for 300 years! Even though the Book of Enoch is not canon (nor am I attempting to make it canon or suggesting that it should be), here is some interesting background from this scholarly work of Dr. Heiser in his book, *Reversing Hermon*:

"The book we know as 1 Enoch was well known to early Christians. This isn't surprising given three transparent facts: (1) 1 Enoch is a substantially pre-Christian literary work that enjoyed readership among Jews in the Second Temple Period; (2) Christianity was born out

7

of Second Temple Judaism; and (3) New Testament writers either presuppose or utilize its content in portions of their own writing."[4]

Though this book is not exclusively about Enoch, it is important to understand the historical context of the writings about Enoch. It is also helpful for building the framework of *walking with God* to see that Enoch was trained to be a voice to his generation during those years that he walked with God. In fact, Jude 1:14-15 actual quotes an entire chapter of the Book of Enoch that shows that Enoch was a prophetic voice to his generation:

> *14 "It was also about these that Enoch, the seventh from Adam, prophesied, saying, "Behold, the Lord comes with ten thousands of his holy ones, 15 to execute judgment on all and to convict all the ungodly of all their deeds of ungodliness that they have committed in such an ungodly way, and of all the harsh things that ungodly sinners have spoken against him."*

Jude 14-15

Enoch's life shows that there is profound truth that comes from understanding and engaging in walking with God. Let us look at the Hebrew definition of *walk* and begin to pull out the hidden treasure that is available to those who are hungry.

H1980 Halak

1) To go, walk, come

1a) (Qal)

1a1) to go, walk, come, depart, proceed, move, and go away

---

[4] Heiser, Michael S. *Reversing Hermon: Enoch, The Watchers & The Forgotten Mission of Jesus Christ*. Bellingham, Washington: Lexham Press, 2015.

1a2) to die, live, manner of life (figuratively)

The Hebrew word for *walk* figuratively means the manner of life that one lives. *Halak* is used several times in Scripture to describe the lifestyle of the people of Israel. The Evangelical Dictionary of Biblical Theology describes *walk* in this fashion:

> "The verb "walk" in its literal sense of going along or moving about on foot at a moderate pace is found numerous times in the Gospels. However, this same verb is often used throughout the Old Testament and the epistles of the New Testament in a metaphorical way. In this sense, it means to follow a certain course of life or to conduct oneself in a certain way. Many times, the verb translated "walk" is present tense in the Greek of the New Testament, which means that the writer is referring to a continued mode of conduct or behavior. In fact, the infinitive "to walk" can be translated in a Hebraist way, "to live." Such a use is common in the Old Testament and the writings of Paul and of John, but is not found in those of Peter or James."[5]

---

[5] Gerig, W. L. (1996). Walk. In Evangelical dictionary of Biblical Theology (electronic ed., p. 806). Grand Rapids: Baker Book House.

Yoked to Walk in Covenant

Now that we have talked briefly about what it means to walk with God let us look at this verse again with a little more understanding:

24 Enoch walked with God, and he was not, for God took him.

Genesis 5:24

Enoch walked with God. This is incredible to think about, especially since Enoch was seven generations removed from Adam. That is, Enoch was seven generations removed from where mankind was put out of the Garden of God (Ezekiel 28:13). It was in the Garden of Eden where the voice of God walked in the cool of the day and because of man's disobedience death entered the earth as man was evicted from the place where God communed with him. Yet despite that, seven generations after that punishment, Enoch was still able to walk with God in a place of intimacy. How did Enoch know about these coming judgments spoken of in Jude? Enoch knew through living in constant relationship and communication with God.

The Hebrew word for God is *Elohim.* Interestingly, *Elohim* is a plural word, yet in this context it is speaking of the one true God. Other places in scripture, the name, *Elohim,* is used for other gods or beings who live in the spiritual realm, but in Genesis 5:24 it is used to describe Yahweh. In the Ancient Hebrew and Semitic translation, Semitic scholar Jeff Benner explains the details about *Elohim* in this fashion:

"The word "el" was originally written with two pictographic letters, one being an ox head

10

and the other a shepherd staff. The ox represented strength and the staff of the shepherd represented authority. First, the Ancient Hebrews saw Elohim as the strong one of authority. The shepherd staff was also understood as a staff on the shoulders, a yoke. Secondly, the Ancient Hebrews saw Elohim as the ox in the yoke. When plowing a field two oxen were placed in a yoke, one was the older more experienced one, and the other was the younger and less experienced. The younger would then learn from the older. The Hebrews saw Elohim as the older experienced ox and they as the younger that learns from him."[6]

An older ox, yoked to a younger ox, taught the younger how to plow the field as they walked together towards a plow mark. It was figurative of the covenant or marriage contract between Yahweh the older ox and Israel the younger ox. According to Benner, the covenant blessing and curses of Deuteronomy 28 () was a picture of this yoking together of Yahweh and Israel in covenant marriage. This picture also describes Enoch walking in covenant with God as the younger ox yoked to Yahweh the older ox. Jesus speaks similar language to His disciples in Matthew 11:27-30:

> [28] *Come to me, all who labor and are heavy laden, and I will give you rest.* [29] *Take my yoke upon you, and learn from me, for I am gentle and lowly in heart, and you will find rest for your souls.* [30] *For my yoke is easy, and my burden is light.*"

---

[6] Jeff Benner. Ancient Hebrew Research Center. Retrieved from: http://www.ancient-hebrew.org/vocabulary_definitions_god.html

Jesus is bringing fresh revelation and truth to what Jeremiah the prophet declared:

> *Thus says the LORD: "Stand by the roads, and look, and ask for the ancient paths, where the good way is; and walk in it, and find rest for your souls. But they said, 'We will not walk in it.'*

Jeremiah 6:17

Incredible! Jesus is calling those who are His disciples to take on His yoke and learn to walk in the ancient path of the way of The Lord. This also indicates that discipleship with Jesus includes walking with Him in intimacy and making a covenant with him to walk in the ancient paths of the God of Israel.

Moving Toward the Plow Mark

A pair of yoked oxen were both plowing towards a destination called the *plow mark*. The Ancient Hebrew Lexicon explains it this way:

> "**Plow/ Mark:** The pictograph of the aleph is a picture of an ox. The tav is a picture of two crossed sticks used to make a *sign or mark*. Combined these pictures represent "*an ox moving toward a mark*". When plowing a field with oxen, *the plowman drives the oxen toward a distant mark* in order to keep the furrow straight. A traveler arrives at his destination by following a *mark*. The traveling toward a mark, destination or person. The arrival of one to the mark. A "you" is an individual who has arrived to a "me". The coming toward a mark. A *standard, or flag, with the family mark hangs as a sign.* An agreement or covenant by two where a sign or

mark of the agreement is made as a reminder to both part."[7]

The Ancient Hebrew concept of the mark was a *plow mark*. The *plow mark* was two crossed sticks that served as the target the ox moved toward or simply *the mark*! First, this mark serves as a sign or a target. Sin means to miss the sign or the mark. Therefore, how can we hit the mark if we cannot see it? The target we are aiming for is to become like Jesus. We must understand the function of the oxen in this regard. For this is the beauty of understanding the older ox (master-teacher) and the younger ox (disciple) picture, with them yoked together, plowing the field, and moving towards a particular mark or destination. That destination is to become conformed to the image of Christ. Thus, the following definition unpacks the metaphorical meaning behind *Elohim*:

Ox Strength: The pictograph the letter *aleph* is a picture of an ox head that also represents its strength. The pictograph of the letter *lamed* is a picture of a shepherd staff and represents the authority of the shepherd. Combined these two pictographs mean *the strong authority* and can be used about anyone or anything having strong authority. The yoke is understood as a *staff on the shoulders* (see Isaiah 9:4), in order to harness power for pulling loads such as a wagon or plow. Hence, the two pictographs can also represent *the ox in the yoke*. Often, two oxen were yoked together. An older, more experienced ox would be teamed up (yoked) with a younger, less experienced ox. ***The older ox in the yoke is the 'strong authority' who, through the yoke, teaches the younger.***

Swear /Yoke or the yoking together of two parties is another picture called on here. A treaty or

---

[7] Jeff Brenner. *Ancient Hebrew Lexicon Bible*, 2004.

covenant binds two parties together through an oath (yoke). The oath included blessings for abiding by the covenant agreement and curses for breaking the covenant (see Deuteronomy 28). *The God of the Hebrews was seen as the older ox who is yoked to his people in a covenant relationship[8].*

The Hebrew word for 'learn' or 'yoke' also originates from this same root. Thus, God is the older ox yoked to us, the inexperienced ox. He is leading and teaching us how to plow the field of our heart and leading us to the plow mark. It is incredible to see that this is also describing the yoked relationship as a marriage covenant between the Yahweh and Israel! Now let us take this concept of being *yoked in marriage covenant"* and view its typology in the relationship between Enoch and God.

Caught Up in Intimacy

Scripture declares that Enoch "was not because God took him." Here is where it gets very interesting. The Hebrew word for "took" is *laquach* which actually means *to snatch and take away a wife and to marry!* Enoch walked with God in daily communion until lastly God took him in marriage or the consummation of covenant! What God did in relation to Enoch was a prophetic picture of what He desired to accomplish with His Bride, Israel, in the Old Testament and it is that same burning passion that Christ the Bridegroom has for His Bride the Church, both Jewish and Gentile.

The yoke is a depiction of marriage and it is figurative of learning. We see this principle in the gospel of Matthew when Jesus declared to his disciples

---

[8] Jeff Brenner. *Ancient Hebrew Lexicon Bible*, 2004.

to, *Take of My yoke and learn from Me* (Matthew 11:29).

There is a profound truth revealed when we understand that the meaning of the name Enoch is to *dedicate* or *initiate,* and it derives from the root word that means *to train or discipline*! Enoch walked with God until Enoch *was not* and in the same way we must walk with Jesus as He trains us, disciples us and we become a *was not,* or simply put they no longer see us but Him only! Just as Enoch walked with God and was continually *raptured* into secret places of intimacy until he disappeared, in similar fashion, we must walk in intimacy and discipleship with Jesus until we disappear and all people can see is Christ in us.

Paul declares that when one turns to the Lord, the veil is taken away and what was hidden is now revealed (2 Corinthians 3:16). The phrase "shall be taken away" is actually one Greek word, which means, "to remove all around, to unveil and cast off an anchor and take away or up". When our Bridegroom reveals Himself to us through intimate communion as we walk with Him, anchors that have kept us *stuck* will begin to be lifted as we are raptured in intimacy with Him. The more He reveals Himself and the more we become like Him, the more completely our mortality is swallowed up the victory of His life (2 Corinthians 5:5; Isaiah 25:8). It is in this secret place of intimacy with him that we learn how to die to self and become His habitation and manifest the fruit of what He reveals.

Noah Walked with God

The Book of Genesis also describes briefly that Noah *walked with God.*

"These are the generations of Noah. Noah was a righteous man, blameless in his generation. Noah walked with God."

Genesis 6:9

When we read the Scripture in context, it reveals that because the sons of God came down and slept with the daughters of men the earth was full of corruption and violence. Giants that were the offspring of sons of God and human women had corrupted the genes of man...yet Noah was blameless. Why and how did Noah stay blameless in midst of corruption where only he and his family were on the Ark when the flood came? It was because Noah walked with God. The constant intimate fellowship and covenant discipleship that Noah experienced with God kept him from the corruption present in the earth. Peter gives a very similar declaration to believers:

> *By which he has granted to us his precious and very great promises, so that through them you may become partakers of the divine nature, having escaped from the world because of sinful desire.*

2 Peter 1:4

Noah, in the midst of a corrupt generation, kept himself in purity and became a prophetic voice of the Lord because he walked with God. Noah became a voice that prepared a generation for the judgment that would come through an event that had never happened before, right up until that point in time. It had never rained on the earth and Noah was given the task to prophesy about an event that had never been seen before. How did Noah move so boldly? It was because Noah walked with God.

16

Chapter 3
Discipleship:
Learning To Walk in the
Kingdom

Now that I have introduced the importance and parallels of the lives of Enoch, Noah and discipleship, I will compare this to what I will refer to as, *The Enoch Principle*, as it related to discipleship training on several levels. I hesitate to use the term "training" because some could interpret this as being separate from intimacy, yet the principle of discipleship training is immersed in intimacy. Enoch walked with Elohim daily in a place of intimacy. The Hebrew meaning of the name Enoch. *Chanak*, as I mentioned previously means *to initiate or discipline*, as well as *to train up*. The book of Proverbs admonishes us to *train up* a child in the *way* he should go so when he matures he will not depart from it (Proverbs 22:6). The phrase used for *training up* a child shares the same root as the name Enoch. In Enoch, we see the principle of being trained up and discipled *in the way of the Lord*. Scripture continually admonishes Israel to walk in His ways, as in the following passages:

*So you shall keep the commandments of the Lord your God by **walking** in **his ways** and by fearing him.*

Deuteronomy 8:6

*"And now, Israel, what does the LORD your God require of you, but to fear the LORD your God, to **walk in all his ways**, to love him, to serve*

*the LORD your God with all your heart and with
all your soul."*

*The Lord will establish you as a people holy to
himself, as he has sworn to you, if you keep the
commandments of the Lord your God and walk in
his ways.*

Deuteronomy 28:9

*Only be very careful to observe the
commandment and the law that Moses the servant
of the LORD commanded you, to love
the LORD your God, and to* **walk in all his ways**
*and to keep his commandments and to cling to
him and to serve him with all your heart and with
all your soul."*

Joshua 22:5

The LORD was with Jehoshaphat, because he
walked *in the earlier ways of his father David.
He did not seek the Baals.*

2 Chronicles 17:3

Walking in His Ways

As we see from just a few examples in the
Scriptures, walking with God also means to walk in His
ways. The ways of God are very significant in
Scripture. The Hebrew word for "ways" is *derek* which
means a road that is *walked* signifying that *ways* are the
lifestyle one lives or *walks*. When we walk in the ways
of God, we are following His commandments, statues
and voice. Walking in His ways is to live a lifestyle that
aligns with His moral character. It is the place where
our hearts have been transformed and the fruit of our
actions give the proof of that.

This is not meant to express a legalistic stance, but rather, one, which reflects someone who is **walking in discipleship** with their teacher. Psalms 103:7 declares that while Israel knew the acts of God, Moses knew His ways. Israel watched the acts of God be displayed through one who knew the ways of God. Moses did not stay at the foot of the mountain when God in His glory came down upon Mount Sinai, but the people of Israel did stay at the foot of the mountain, terrified by the Presence of God. We see that Moses, on the other hand, entered into the cloud and communed with God, in order to see His form and hear His voice. It was in this place of communion and intimacy Moses that was trained as a leader to know the ways of the Lord; Israel, with the exception of Joshua, chose to receive it second hand from Moses because of their fear. We are no longer standing at the foot of the Mount Sinai, as the writer of Hebrews declares, but we are invited to Mount Zion to be taught and trained in the Presence of the Lord.

Walking In the Way of the King

The truth that I want to communicate regarding the life of Enoch and the disciples walking with Jesus is revealed as we look at the correlation of the meaning of the Hebrew words for *walk* and *kingdom*. The Hebrew words for kingdom, *mamlakah* and messenger *malak,* both come from the same root word for walk *halak* which means a person's walk or daily lifestyle. One of the meanings of *malak* or *messenger* is *"a theophanic messenger or God manifesting in the form of a message through the messenger."* This word also speaks of one who operates as an ambassador sent from another country to walk for another. It is interesting to note that one of the Hebrew words for *work* is *melakah,* which shares the same root and it is interpreted as a *message through action.*

The most profound place where the disciples saw the kingdom manifested in the life of Jesus was not in His miracles, signs and wonders, but in His daily walk! The kingdom of God must first be manifested or *seen* in our walk or lifestyle, where the fruit and actions of our life are a reflection of the Jesus we preach. Jesus Himself said that He is *The Way, the Truth, and the Life and no one comes to the Father except through Him"* (John 14:6).

Walking with Jesus, then, is to be discipled in the way of truth that releases life and leads us to the Father. The disciples learned how to manifest the kingdom by walking with the King and watching His daily life. . I believe this is why they desired for Jesus to teach them how to pray—because they had experienced how profound His daily prayer life was. God is engaging us to learn how to walk out messages in discipleship with Jesus, so that we can be sent forth as a message and witness of the very life of Jesus!

This was the journey of the disciples of the Lamb as they transitioned from disciples to apostles! That's why the book of Acts declares with great power that they were *witnesses of His resurrection* (Acts 4:33) and why Paul declares to the church in Corinth that we are to be ambassadors of Messiah (2 Corinthians 5:20). This does not mean that all of us are called to be apostles, but we are all called to be disciples, to walk with Jesus until His life becomes our life, and we are sent forth as witnesses that He is alive in us!

The Death Walk of Discipleship

The transition and radical transformation of the disciples of the Lamb from the time before the crucifixion of Jesus to his appearing to them again in the upper room in the book of Acts can only be understood by recalling that they walked with Jesus during his time of ministry on the earth. The Holy Spirit came to bring revelation of all that Jesus taught them during their time with Him. It is significant to see that another meaning of the word walk in Greek is "to die," as well as the root of the word apostle in Greek, which means "to cease to exist." As Jesus walked with His disciples and was training them to be His apostles and ambassadors, they were walking out his message by learning to die to their preconceived notions of what the Messiah would look like and how He would operate when He came. This was necessary so that they could represent or re-present Him accurately to the world.

Jesus was yoked together with them in covenant, as their teacher, leading them to experience death to self through Him, so that they would become vessels able to display His resurrection life through both word and deed. The discipleship was necessary not simply in order to perform miracles, heal the sick, and cast out devils—for they were already doing that before the cross (Matthew 10:1-3)—but rather, it was necessary in order to re-present Him as King and manifest the government of His kingdom on earth as it is in heaven. To accomplish this, Jesus gives His disciples some clear directives regarding what He requires from them in the Gospel of Luke:

> And he said to all, "If anyone would come after me, let him deny himself and take up his cross daily and follow me. For whoever would save his life will lose it, but whoever loses his life for my sake will save it. For what does it profit a man if he gains the whole world and loses or forfeits himself? For whoever is ashamed of me and of my words, of him will the Son of Man be

ashamed when he comes in his glory and the glory of the Father and of the holy angels.

Luke 9:23-26

Those clear directives included the following: (1) denying ourselves, (2) taking up our cross daily and this is what it means to (3) follow Him. The Greek word for "follow" is *akoloutheo* and is defined as, *being in the same way with, to join and become his disciple* (Strong's Concordance). The price of becoming a follower of Christ is not for the faint of heart! To deny yourself means to utterly deny, disown and disdain oneself. It carries the meaning of affirming that there is no longer any acquaintance or connection with who you were and that now you have lost sight of your own self and your own interest. Secondly, Theologian Albert Barnes describes taking up the cross in this way:

> "When persons were condemned to be crucified, a part of the sentence was that they should carry the cross on which they were to die to the place of execution. Thus, Christ carried his, until he fainted from fatigue and exhaustion. Matthew 27:31. The cross was usually composed of two rough beams of wood, united in the form of this figure of a cross for it was an instrument of death. Matthew 27:31-32.

> To carry it was burdensome, was disgraceful, was trying to the feelings, was an addition to the punishment. Therefore, "to carry the cross" is a figurative expression, denoting that we must endure whatever is burdensome, or is trying, or is considered disgraceful, in following Christ. It consists simply in doing our duty, let the people of the world think of it or speak of it as they may. It does not consist

22

in making trouble for ourselves, or doing things merely "to be opposed;" it is doing just what is required of us in the Scriptures, let it produce whatever shame, disgrace, or pain it may. This every follower of Jesus is required to do."[9]

Death to False Perceptions and Comfort Zones

The journey of discipleship and walking with Jesus, the lover of our souls, is one of continually casting away of false perceptions that have built false realities of who He is and ultimately who we are. John the Apostle penned the statement that helps us understand the power of having the right perception of who we are and will be:

> *2 Beloved, we are God's children now, and what we will be has not yet appeared; but we know that when he appears we shall be like him, because we shall see him as he is. 3 And everyone who thus hopes in him purifies Himself as he is pure.*
>
> 1 John 3:2-3

As we continually abide and walk with God, there is a powerful transformation taking place. Our perceptions have the power to free us, as well as the power to imprison us. Perception is the ability to see, hear, or become aware of something through the senses. Perception is the flow of information received from the five senses to the brain to help us interpret the present

---

[9] Albert Barnes Commentary on The Whole Book of Matthew. Retrieved from:
https://www.studylight.org/commentaries/bnb/matthew.html

world. What we perceive and how we perceive it affects our daily lifestyle. Perception creates a reality or worldview and culture that becomes our comfort zone.

Our comfort zone is a psychological, emotional, and behavioral construct that defines the routine of our daily life[10]. Being in one's comfort zone implies familiarity, safety, and security. It describes the patterned world of our existence, keeps us calm and free from anxiety, as well as creating a healthy adaptation for our lives[11]. Psychologist Abigail Brenner also states that stepping out of our comfort zone when it is time to transition into what is coming next, will bring growth and transformation[12]. If this is the understanding of the power of perception from an emotional, behavioral, and psychological standpoint, then it is imperative to grasp the reality of walking with God in a spiritual reality such that every step with Him and in him brings us out of our comfort zones.

When we walk by faith, it is walking in the spiritual reality that what is now seen was not made out of things that are visible (Hebrews 11:3). It having the revelation of Jesus Christ frame our worldview and destroy constructs of comfort that are based on a reality founded in a worldview that is not conducive to kingdom culture. Our new perception of Him, then becomes the blueprint from which we build our lives personally, as sons of God.

---

[10] Abigail Brenner M.D. 2015. "5 Benefits of Stepping Out of Your Comfort Zone". Psychology Today.
[11] Ibid.
[12] Ibid.

Whoever makes a practice of sinning is of the devil, for the devil has been sinning from the beginning. The reason the Son of God appeared was to destroy the works of the devil.

1 John 3:8

Furthermore, it is the revelation of Christ that destroys constructs of religion that have built their own version of Jesus and formed Him according to their own imagination. It is the appearing of Christ, which destroys the works of the devil (I John 3:8). The works of man's hands in attempting to form a version of Jesus and the kingdom that fits within their comfort zone is the very lie that keeps many in bondage, although most are not even conscious of it. Walking with God brings a personal revival and awakening to who He is and frees us from bondages of constructs and systems of false kingdoms that leads us away from our inheritance. The word "destroy" in 1 John 3:8 is the Greek word *luo* which means, "to loosen, break, destroy, dissolve," as well as, "set free.[13]" Thayer's definition is "to lose any person bound with chains, or law and binding force, to do away with, to deprive of authority.[14] " *Luo* also means, "to declare unlawful," which has incredible implications in the context of breaking out of our comfort zones. *Luo* is used in Matthew 16:19, which we discussed earlier regarding the keys to the kingdom being for binding and loosing. We walk the death walk of discipleship, in that with every revelation of Christ, every step we take must be a death to self and a destruction of false constructs, as well as resulting freedom from the laws connected to it. Every construct is a system or kingdom that brings a level of bondage we are unconscious of until revelation comes. However,

---

[13] Strong's Lexicon Dictionary.
[14] Thayer's New Testament Dictionary.

when the plumb line revelation of the King arrives, we die to ourselves and are freed from that world and that's how we begin to enter greater realities of the kingdom. The works of the devil are destroyed as we walk daily in Jesus, who is The Way, The Truth, and The Life (John 14:6).

Enoch and Jesus: Messengers of Yahweh

The depiction of Enoch walking with God as the younger ox is a profound parallel of the disciples walking with Jesus, which in turn gives us an incredible portrait of personal discipleship, as we walk with Jesus. As I briefly discussed earlier, the Hebrew word for "angel or messenger" is *malak*, which derives from the root word *halak* or *walk*. *Malak* and *mamlakah* 'kingdom' derive from the word that means 'to walk among the people.' The meaning reflects when the king stands up from his throne and walks among the people; it is a visible demonstration of him extending his rule. Thus, *kingdom* also means *dominion*. As we walk in discipleship with the King, His rule extends into every area of our lives, until He has full dominion in us through our continued submission and obedience. The significance of the connection between these three words—walk, messenger, and kingdom—is found in the goal of our being disciples of Jesus and manifesting His nature as ambassadors.

Scripture tells us that Enoch walked in union with God for 300 years until he was not found, because God took him. Enoch prophetically represents those who walk with Christ daily, pick up their crosses and follow His ways, because they are not just receiving the message of the King but also becoming a message themselves. It is in the death walk of the first disciples that as they walked with Jesus, they also began to cease

26

to exist and became witnesses of His resurrection. This is the call of all believers regardless of whether one is called to fivefold ministry leadership or not. We are all called to be conformed to the image of Christ and it is by walking with Him that we begin to have fellowship with His sufferings and experience the power of His resurrection.

Chapter 4
Witnesses of His Resurrection and Ambassadors of the King

The purpose of discipleship with Jesus is to be conformed into His image, as the Last Adam, Jesus, comes to bring us back into conformity with the function of the first Adam, as God's image bearers. The process the disciples endured in walking in Jesus before the crucifixion and their incredible ministry and apostolic functions after His ascension give us a picture of the maturation of discipleship—that is, how to mature as a disciple. It is one thing to have the authority to cast out demons, heal the sick, cleanse the leper, and raise the dead and it is another thing to experience being transformed into His image. Even with this authority given to them by Jesus in Matthew 10, we still find that one is a devil (Judas); one denies Him three times (Peter); others encountered demons they could not cast out. All of them still did not understand much of Jesus' teachings, right up until the time the Holy Spirit came and brought transformational revelation. We have accounts of disciples releasing signs and wonders, and Jesus declaring that many will come in saying they have done the same kinds of things. But, His response will be, "I never knew you. Depart from me you workers of lawlessness!" Discipleship is not just about our actions, but it is about our inner character being conformed to His image.

In the book of Acts, the transformation of the apostles and the impact of their testimony and ministry are astounding. The very same apostles who were hiding when Jesus was resurrected are the same ones who moved in boldness, proclaiming the resurrection of

Jesus, in the face of persecution and death. The Holy Spirit breathed into them, baptized them, and brought the revelation of Jesus and all that He taught them during the time they walked with him and did life together. The phrase Luke uses to describe the apostles in the midst of persecution accurately describes the transformation of the apostles had undergone:

33 And with great power, the apostles gave witness to the resurrection of the Lord Jesus. And great grace was upon them all.

Acts 4:33

Luke declares that the apostles did not go witness that Jesus was alive through words alone, but they gave witness to the resurrection. The Greek word for *witness* can sometimes be translated as 'testimony,' as well, so it can also mean that the apostles gave testimony to the resurrection of the Lord Jesus. Previously, in the same chapter, as educated Pharisees observed Peter and John, they were perplexed that even though they were untrained and uneducated according to their religious standards, the Pharisees KNEW that the apostles had been with Jesus! Something about the "walk" of the apostles indicated to others they had been with Jesus. Jesus may not physically be in the earth anymore, but He is being seen in the actions of His disciples who have now become witnesses and testimonies that He is alive in them!

The Greek word for 'witness' is *marturion* and it means *evidence given. Marturion* derives from the word *martus,* which is defined as,

"...a witness in a legal sense in a courtroom, in a historical sense one who was a spectator at an event or contest, in an ethical sense, those who after His example have proved the

30

strength and genuineness of their faith in
Christ by undergoing a violent death."[15]

In 2 Thessalonians 1:10, the testimony of Paul
and the others did not just come through their
proclamation of the gospel, but also through the fact
that they borne witness of the power of the gospel. The
disciples became legal witnesses of the resurrection of
Christ. Their characters were so transformed by
becoming partakers of His divine nature that they borne
witness of the very life of Jesus, which was
demonstrated in and through them. The power of Jesus
moving in them, then, was proof that He was not in the
grave, but alive in His representatives, that is, the
church. The apostles were vessels that were re-
presenting Jesus and they were living embodiments and
testimonies that victory over death and Satan was
accomplished through Jesus' death, burial, resurrection,
and ascension. The advancement of the kingdom had
begun, and the early church, with great grace upon
them, was a legal witness of that victory.

Ambassadors of Christ

With the start of the outpouring of the Holy Spirit
and the inauguration of the kingdom of heaven on earth,
Paul began to describe the importance of what it means
to re-present Christ on earth:

*Therefore, if anyone is in Christ, he is a new
creation. The old has passed away; behold, the
new has come. All this is from God, who through
Christ reconciled us to himself and gave us the
ministry of reconciliation; that is, in Christ God
was reconciling the world to himself, not counting*

---

[15] Strong's Concordance Lexicon Dictionary.

their trespasses against them, and entrusting to us the message of reconciliation. Therefore, we are ambassadors for Christ, God making his appeal through us. We implore you on behalf of Christ, be reconciled to God. For our sake, he made him to be sin who knew no sin, so that in him we might become the righteousness of God.

2 Corinthians 5:17-21

As we walk with Christ in discipleship, we are entering into union with Him. In doing so, we die to self, cease to exist, and His nature begins to be manifested in and through us. Christ modeled the ministry of reconciliation for us, as the Father was in Christ, reconciling the world to Himself. Jesus was the visible manifestation of the invisible God and the express image of the Father, (Colossians 1:15; Hebrews 1:3). Paul goes so far as to say that Christ was the firstborn of many brethren. That means that as joint heirs with our elder brother, Jesus, we also share in manifesting the nature of the Father. This is not to say we are elite and equal with Jesus, but rather, that we are becoming vessels filled with His nature.

Jesus the Apostle, was an ambassador of the Kingdom who declared, "When you see Me you have seen the Father" (John 14:10). Paul proclaims that just as Jesus represented the Father to people of the world, the believer, in his role as a new creation in Christ, stands in the place of Christ, declaring to the world, "Be reconciled to God." The believer operates as the ambassador of the King, which also means as an ambassador of the kingdom. An ambassador is one who is a representative sent from a foreign country to represent their country. When the ambassador arrives, they are not treated merely as an individual representative. For example, let's say I am an ambassador of the United States and I am assigned to

France. The French government will not interact with me just as the ambassador of the United States, but rather, as the ambassador, I would be seen AS the United States, because when ambassadors are seen and treated as the nation they represent.

In the passage above from 2 Corinthians, Paul likens the ministry of reconciliation to that of ambassadors. This means that as Christ's ambassadors, when people see us, they should see Christ—the one we represent! One of the definitions of *messengers* in the Hebrew, which derives from the word *walk,* as previously discussed, also means *to be an ambassador.* The Greek root word of ambassador is *presbuteros,* meaning, *elderly, older, senior, or one who is part of a presbytery.* This definition alludes to the fact that only mature individuals can properly re-present Christ. This reveals that the goal of discipleship is to become a mature ambassador of the King, as an instrument and vessel for reconciling people to the King.

Authentic Discipleship

The goal of all believers is to become a representation and image-bearer of Christ in our daily lifestyles and the means to accomplish that end is through discipleship. It is imperative that five-fold ministry leaders and elders first become mature ambassadors in order to be able to model and lead others to maturity within the body of Christ. Then it will be possible for the church to collectively begin to take up its role as an embassy in a foreign land, an embassy that demonstrates the kingdom of heaven on earth. The goal of believers is maturity; that is, to be mature image-bearers of Christ in order to win souls to Him through our words and deeds. Discipleship cannot just consist of teaching people how to operate in

33

charismatic gifts while leaving them immature in their obedience to our Lord and the sanctification he desires.

In the charismatic-Pentecostal realms, much (but certainly not all) of the discipleship training given focuses on training people how to prophecy, cast out demons, heal the sick, and move in miracles. Rarely do we see discipleship training where mature fathers and mothers in the faith are walking with sons and daughters in the faith, dealing with transforming their character, along with emotional and spiritual development, so that they are mature and responsible enough to move in those charismatic gifts or in leadership roles with appropriate responsibility. Discipleship is not a just a six to nine week training where you can receive a certificate that states you can now prophesy and heal the sick, but rather, it is a life long journey of dying to self and becoming like Jesus, in order to properly re-present Him with integrity.

Discipleship is about true intimacy where through the Holy Spirit fathers and mothers of the faith see into the dark, hidden places of our hearts to expose, cleanse, crush, tear down, and uproot idols and vain imaginations that produce false ideals and cultures that are not in conformity with Christ's kingdom. True discipleship occurs when the power of the kingdom is manifest in our hearts, resulting in the destruction of the false kingdoms of this world and its cultures. This kind of discipleship based on the revelation of Christ creates a kingdom culture where people can be cultivated and grow. Walking with Christ in discipleship includes our daily walk with Him, as well as with those leaders He has called to help shape and conform us into His image.

In fact, the prophetic picture of Enoch and Noah walking with God himself does not give us license to say that we can just be discipled by God himself and that we do not need leaders and community. That is a false assumption that will hinder spiritual growth. First, we need to recall that the culture of God's people has been one of community from the beginning, as each father was teacher and leader in his own household, orally passing on their history and traditions to their children. Deuteronomy 6:7 instructs fathers to diligently teach their children by repeating and reiterating the nature of God. Secondly, the perfect picture of discipleship is not Enoch, but Jesus, God in the flesh, modeling discipleship through his interactions with the apostles, who in turn would model it in the same manner, discipling nations. Jesus is the perfect Son, who manifested the nature of the Father as He trained His disciples to walk as He walked, as they became able to function as mature apostles and ambassadors. Next, we will take a deeper look at what is was like to walk with Jesus and do life together and what lessons can we glean from the gospels in order to better understand walking with God in discipleship.

Chapter 5
Discipleship: Walking in the Council of the Lord

One of the most important truths of walking with the Lord in discipleship is walking in His divine council. There are powerful parallels of revelation that are seen when comparing the language of the relationship of the Old Testament prophets and God with Jesus and His disciples. In The Book of Jeremiah, God addresses the false prophets and makes a clear distinction between the true and the false:

"For who among them has stood in the council of the Lord to see and to hear his word, or who has paid attention to his word and listened"?

Jeremiah 23:16

According to the word of the Lord from Jeremiah, what distinguishes true prophets from false prophets was true prophets stood in the council of the Lord. Those who spoke for God had to meet Him and receive instructions and directives from His divine council. The Hebrew word *sod* means *council,* is that is, a secret and divine council. Browns Drivers Briggs defines *sod* as, "council, counsel, assembly or divan (a legislative body), circle of familiar friends, intimacy with God." It is also used in the Book of Amos:

"For the Lord God does nothing without revealing his secret to his servants the prophets."

Amos 3:7

Amos declares that God does nothing until He reveals His *sod* or divine council to His servants the prophets. *Council* differs from *counsel* in that the word *counsel* is to give or receive wisdom and advice, whereas *council* means to be part of the judicial, governmental, and legislative company to institutes laws. The council of the Lord is the judicial and legislative decisions Yahweh has made from His throne. We get the opportunity to peer into His council in 1 Kings 22 when Ahab and Jehoshaphat inquire of Micaiah to see whether the Lord will give them victory if they go to battle:

> *And Micaiah said, "Therefore hear the word of the LORD: I saw the LORD sitting on his throne, and all the host of heaven standing beside him on his right hand and on his left; and the LORD said, 'Who will entice Ahab, that he may go up and fall at Ramoth-gilead?' And one said one thing, and another said another. Then a spirit came forward and stood before the LORD, saying, 'I will entice him.' And the LORD said to him, 'By what means?' And he said, 'I will go out, and will be a lying spirit in the mouth of all his prophets.' And he said, 'You are to entice him, and you shall succeed; go out and do so.' Now therefore behold, the LORD has put a lying spirit in the mouth of all these your prophets; the LORD has declared disaster for you."*

1 Kings 22:19-23

Micaiah begins to describe a heavenly scene where Yahweh is sitting on the throne surrounded by all the host of heaven and Yahweh asked who would entice Ahab that he may fall? What is Micaiah seeing in the Spirit? He is gazing into the heavenly council around the throne of God to hear what His decree is regarding Ahab. The passage in Amos showed that God would do nothing until He reveals His secret council *sod* to His servants the prophets. In the narrative in 1 Kings,

Micaiah is leaning in to see, to hear the council of the Lord, and then as a mouthpiece and messenger to release the authority of the verdict to Ahab. It did not matter that four hundred other prophets told Ahab that He would be victorious, for the legislative council from the throne of the Lord declared otherwise.

Intimacy Gives Us Access

Notice that when we talk about the council of the Lord, by definition we are also talking about intimacy. Prior to Amos 3:3 states, "How can two walk together unless they agree?" This denotes two who are walking together and doing life together, as they are coming into a place of union that flows out of intimacy. It is agreement that flows out of doing life together. The first revelatory truth to grasp from walking in His council is that He reveals His secrets to those who are intimate with Him. Agreement that flows out of intimacy derives from a place of trust, because the two who walk together are doing life together. The Book of Job uses this word *council* in an interesting way in the context of Job's friend Eliphaz asking him some intriguing questions:

> *"Are you the first man who was born? Or were you brought forth before the hills? Have you listened in the council of God? And do you limit wisdom to yourself?"*
>
> Job 15:7-8

Of course, Job was not the first man, for we know Adam was. So Eliphaz is alluding to the fact that Adam listened to the council of God. As Adam walked with God in the Garden of Eden, it was where His divine council was. The council of God is a physical place, but where God's dwelling place is…that is where

His council is. Dr. Michael Heiser says this regarding God's dwelling place as it compares to walking:

> "Think back to Genesis 3:8, a passage I've alluded to before, in which Yahweh approaches humans as a man. When Adam and Eve violated God's command, they suddenly heard "the sound of the LORD God walking in the garden in the cool of the day." This "walking" terminology suggests that God appeared to them in human form (spirits don't "walk"). The text says that Adam and Eve knew it was God— there was no surprise or shock. This was an experience they had had before. Adam and Eve were familiar with being in God's presence. The description of Yahweh "walking" also describes God's active presence inside Israel's tabernacle, creating another link between Eden, the cosmic mountain, and the tabernacle sanctuary. One can read the Old Testament in vain for any instance where Yahweh walked around the camp of Israel, as opposed to appearing in a cloud over the holy of holies, and so the description here is not describing God literally glad-handing with the Israelites. Rather, the language is another way of saying that Yahweh's abode was among the Israelites— and where Yahweh's house was, his council was. On the other side of the veil was where Yahweh and his council could be found."[16]

This is profound when we draw the correlation between walking with God and His divine council. If

[16] Heiser, Michael S... 2015. The Unseen Realm: Recovering the Supernatural Worldview of the Bible. Bellingham: Lexham Press. Accessed March 21, 2019

walking with God refers to someone who abides in His Presence, then it gives greater significance to being the house or dwelling place of God. God's council is where His house is. Thus, if we are walking with God, He is also walking with us, and among, meaning that we ourselves are the place of His council.

Jesus and the Full Council of the Father

The powerful truth and correlation between discipleship and walking with God is that *walking* denotes presence. Therefore, walking with God indicates continually abiding in His Presence in order to learn. Prophetically speaking, the life of Enoch, concerning walking with God in discipleship, parallels in several ways the life of the disciples as they walked with Jesus. Recall that Enoch's name means, "*to dedicate and train*," and comes from the Hebrew word *chanak* which means, *to initiate, train up, or discipline.* Enoch was living out his name, while learning and being trained in the ways of the Lord and maintaining the attitude of being yoked to Yahweh the older ox. This idea of discipleship and being yoked to an older teacher or master was part of the culture of the Jewish people.

The Jewish Master-Disciple Relationship

The relationship of the Jewish Rabbis or masters to their disciples can be seen in the relationship of Jesus *the Rabbi* with His disciples. While there are similarities in the comparison, there are also some clear differences, which contributed to the hostile response of the Pharisees and other Jewish leaders of Jesus' day. The relationship between the Master and the disciple was that the Master was a teacher of the Oral Traditions or Oral Torah, which was believed to be the interpretation of the Written Torah. Tradition says that Moses received both the Written and Oral Torah on Mount Sinai and the Oral Torah was passed down from Moses to Joshua to the elders and all the way down to the Rabbis who are the teachers of the Torah[17].

> "One who was devoted to Torah became implicated and obligated to carry it out—to embody it in such a way as to make it become visible to others, as expressed in the rabbinic text: Just as fire leaves a mark upon the body of one who works with it, so the words of Torah leave a mark upon the body of one who works with them. Just as those who work with fire are recognizable, so disciples of the wise are recognized by their manner of walking, by their speech, and by their dress in the market place (SifDeut343)."[18]

When a prospective disciple would come into covenant with a master, several important points were present:

- They memorized their master's words.
- They adopted their master's interpretation of scripture.
- They imitated his ministry model.
- They multiplied his teachings in their own disciples.

---

[17] Neudecker, Reinhard. "Master-Disciple/Disciple-Master Relationship in Rabbinic Judaism and in the Gospels." *Gregorianum* 80, no. 2 (1999): 245-61. http://www.jstor.org/stable/23580264
[18] Ibid.

According to the Mishna, which was one of commentaries of the Oral Traditions, the yoke was the covenant of Torah:

> "Rabbi Nechunia son of Hakanah said, "Anyone who accepts upon himself the yoke of Torah removes from himself the yoke of government duties and the yoke of the way of the world; but one who casts off the yoke of Torah accepts upon himself the yoke of government and the yoke of the way of the world." *Pirkei Avot* 3:5

Jesus declared, "Take of My yoke upon you and learn from Me; for I am meek and lowly in heart, and you will find rest for your souls. For My yoke is easy and My burden is light." (Matthew 11:29-30)

What is this yoke that Jesus is referring to and what is its connection to learning and rest? The yoke, just as we discussed previously in connection with Enoch being yoked to Elohim as a younger ox, that yoke, figuratively speaking, is of labor or service for someone. According to Barnes, yokes can represent:

- Bondage of slavery (Leviticus 26:13; Deuteronomy 28:38)
- Afflictions or crosses (Lamentations 3:27)
- Punishment of sin (Lamentations 1:14)
- Commandments of God or legal ceremonies (Acts 15:10; Galatians 5:1)[19].

Barnes goes on to argue that the *yoke* refers to the religion of the Redeemer and that the disciples should embrace his system of religion and obey him, for religion implies restraint[20]. If the older ox is leading the

---

[19] Barnes, Albert (1962). *Barnes' Notes on the New Testament* (Complete and unabridged in one volume). *Grand Rapids, Michigan*: Kregel Publications. *ISBN 9780825493713*.

younger ox to plow the field, the younger ox is under the lead and restraint of the older ox. The correlation between yoke and rest would seem to be that as we are led of Christ we plowing through the fields of our hearts, removing thorns, thistles and stones out of our hearts, while His leading and teaching restrains our passion. Being yoked, then, is being led to walk in His moral character and learning the art of submission.

The yoke of Jesus was to teach His disciples the revelation of Torah in his role as the New Moses. Moses prophesied of this in Deuteronomy18:5, when he declared that 'God would raise up a Prophet from among them who would be like him.' The importance of this truth is that during the time of Jesus, the Pharisees were thought to be masters of the Oral Traditions that started with Moses. Jesus came to fulfill the written Torah by bringing the right interpretation, which in turn meant the rejection of the old Oral Traditions. The Oral Traditions caused Israel not to recognize the very Messiah they had waited so long for. Jesus spoke of these Oral Traditions when He declared that the word of God has no effect through their traditions (Matthew 15:6). This was a major reason why it was necessary for John the Baptist to come first, because he had to prepare the way for Israel to recognize their Messiah.

Walking in the Council of the Lord

Now that we have compared the life of Enoch as he walked with God, along with the relationship of master-disciple in Jewish culture, we can unpack some powerful revelatory truths that are carried over from Jewish culture into kingdom culture. Jesus declared that

---

[20] Ibid.

the ecclesia would be built on the revelation of who He was, and that judicial and legislative decisions made at the gates of hell would not prevail against it. Jesus was training His disciples to do as He had done, and make disciples of the nations that would be an extension of Himself. I believe it is significant that we are called the *body of Christ*. According to Paul in Ephesians 1, the ecclesia is Jesus' body:

> *And hath put all things under his feet, and gave him to be the head over all things to the church (ecclesia), which is his body, the fullness of him that filleth all in all.*

Ephesians 1:22-23

Previously in this book I referred to the fact that the Hebrew word for kingdom *mamlakah* actually derives from "*halak*" 'walk.' or. The meaning comes from the idea of the king who walks among his people. The word for angel, messenger or ambassador *malak* is also related to *kingdom* and *walk,* in that the definition is "one who walks for another, a messenger or theophanic angel or God coming in the form of an angel or messenger." The call of discipleship with Jesus is to walk out the message of the kingdom with the King until the disciples become witnesses of His resurrection and ambassadors of the kingdom of heaven. Enoch walked with God until He was not seen any longer because God took Him. Likewise, the disciples walked with Jesus until He was not seen any longer because God took him. But he only disappeared so that Jesus could be seen in and through his disciples.

Jesus the Council of the Lord

As discussed previously, *sod* 'council' refers to the secret and divine council of Yahweh. Jesus, who is Yahweh in the flesh, taught His disciples differently than He taught the crowds, as we see in the narrative of the gospels:

> *¹⁰ Then the disciples came and said to him, "Why do you speak to them in parables?" ¹¹ And he answered them, "To you it has been given to know the secrets of the kingdom of heaven, but to them it has not been given.*
>
> Matthew 13:10-11

Jesus taught the crowds in parables, which was a fulfillment of Psalms 78, as well. A parable was a story with a hidden meaning or moral within it, which had the purpose of teaching and instruction. When Jesus taught the parable of the seed and sower, even the disciples did not understand it. Then the disciples pull Jesus aside and ask Him to explain the meaning of the parable. His response is, 'It is given to you to know the mysteries of the kingdom of heaven.' Let us first look at the essence of His statement, which once again indicates that intimacy is the key to understanding the mysteries of the kingdom of heaven. All of the Synoptic gospels record this dialogue with Jesus, which is evidence that it is important to understand the meaning of the parable. The parable itself was a seed that contained the seed of the truth that would produce a harvest in the life of the disciple who disciplined his life by it. The mystery of the kingdom of heaven was hidden or concealed in the narrative of the parable and Jesus only revealed it to those yoked to Him in discipleship.

The Greek word for *mystery* is a powerful word when understood within the context of revelation about the life and culture of the kingdom of heaven. Vine's Dictionary defines mystery as:

> "musterion (3466), primarily that which is known to the mustes, "the initiated" (from mueo, "to initiate into the mysteries"; cf. Phil. 4:12, mueomai, "I have learned the secret," RV). In the NT it denotes, not the mysterious (as with the Eng. word), but that which, being outside the range of unassisted natural apprehension, can be made known only by divine revelation, and is made known in a manner and at a time appointed by God, and to those only who are illumined by His Spirit. In the ordinary sense a "mystery" implies knowledge withheld; its Scriptural significance is truth revealed. Hence, the terms especially associated with the subject are "made known," "manifested," "revealed," "preached," "understand," "dispensation."

> The definition given above may be best illustrated by the following passage: "the mystery which hath been hid from all ages and generations: but now hath it been manifested to His saints" (Col. 1:26, RV). "It is used of:

> "(a) Spiritual truth generally, as revealed in the gospel, 1 Cor. 13:2; 14:2 [cf. 1 Tim. 3:9]. Among the ancient Greeks 'the mysteries' were religious rites and ceremonies practiced by secret societies into which anyone who so desired might be received. Those who were initiated into these 'mysteries' became possessors of certain knowledge, which was not imparted to the uninitiated, and were called

'the perfected,' cf. 1 Cor. 2:6-16 where the
Apostle has these 'mysteries' in mind and
presents the gospel in contrast thereto; here
'the perfected' are, of course the believers"[21].

The mysteries of the kingdom are spiritual truths
that are revealed to the believer who has been initiated
through intimacy. The name Enoch also means,
initiated, so we can conclude that disciples are initiated
into spiritual truths, which bring transformation through
their walking with Jesus. Thayer's defines mystery as
"secret will of God and secret counsels which govern
God in dealing with the righteous, which are hidden
from ungodly and wicked men but plain to the godly."
The Abbott-Smith Manual Greek Lexicon of the New
Testament equates the word 'mystery' or *musterion*
with the Hebrew word for 'secret council' or *sod*[22]. This
is a profound truth if you have been following me up to
this point. If Jesus is Yahweh in the flesh, then the
disciples are walking in the very council (*sod*-secret
council-mystery-*musterion*) of God!

Walking with the Holy Spirit

The picture of Jesus teaching His disciples how to
walk as He walked is preparation for what the Holy
Spirit would come afterwards to bring into full
manifestation:

> [15] *"If you love me, you will keep my*
> *commandments.* [16] *And I will ask the Father, and*

---

[21] Vine, W. E., Merrill F. Unger, William White, and W. E. Vine.
1985. Vine's Complete Expository Dictionary of Old and New
Testament Words. Nashville: Nelson.
[22] G. Abbott-Smith 1922 Abbott-Smith Manual Greek Lexicon of
the New Testament. D.D. D.C.L. T & T Clarke, London.

he will give you another Helper, to be with you
forever, [17] even the Spirit of truth, whom the
world cannot receive, because it neither sees him
nor knows him. You know him, for he dwells with
you and will be in you."

John 14:15-17

Jesus proclaims to His disciples that after His Ascension to the Father when the Holy Spirit comes they will not only do what He did but they will do greater works (John 14:12). Notice the language of Jesus throughout this narrative, for it is striking. He reveals that the Holy Spirit will not dwell with them, but *in* them! While Jesus walked with them and revealed the kingdom, it was not until the Holy Spirit came into them that revelation of all they received from Jesus began to come alive. We may not have had the privilege of walking with Jesus, but because of His death, burial, and resurrection we have the honor of having Him walk *in* us.

Chapter 6
Kingdom Culture, *Ekklesia* and Discipleship

As the disciples walked with Jesus the King, they were learning the laws, protocols, and ways of the life of the kingdom, which is the life of the Spirit. The profound truth about *walking* being the root to kingdom life was first witnessed by the disciples, who saw the kingdom manifested in the daily lifestyle of Jesus. The Great Commission is not just about discipleship of individuals, but also about the discipling of nations, because you cannot shift the beliefs of man without shifting the beliefs of the culture. Individual discipleship is a great place to begin, but it must extend to transforming the culture.

Kingdom Culture and *Ekklesia*

> *16 Simon Peter replied, "You are the Christ, the Son of the living God." 17 And Jesus answered him, "Blessed are you, Simon Bar-Jonah! For flesh and blood has not revealed this to you, but my Father who is in heaven. 18 And I tell you, you are Peter, and on **this rock**, I will build my church, and the gates of hell shall not prevail against it. 19 I will give you the **keys of the kingdom** of heaven, and whatever you bind on earth shall be bound in heaven, and whatever you loose on earth shall be loosed in heaven."*
>
> Matthew 16:16-19

That passage, recorded in Matthew 16, is one the most powerful conversations Jesus had with His disciples regarding His intentions for them as His disciples. The word translated *church* is the Greek word *ekklesia,* which means more than just a gathering of believers. The *ekklesia* are more than just *called out ones*. The *ekklesia* are those called out of darkness and called into becoming the judicial and legislative apostolic embassy that will carry out the commandments of the King. The *ekklesia* becomes the embassy from which ambassadors who re-present Christ establish the laws of the kingdom of heaven on earth. In the Greek culture, *ekklesia* were citizens called to be part of the judicial council. What judicial decrees are they making? The Law of the Spirit of the Life of Jesus. The Law of Liberty and the plumb line that will bring everything which is out of alignment into its proper place. An apostolic company comes into cities, regions, and nations in order to cause the conquered area to look like heaven.

This is the essence of discipleship...teaching the kingdom so the being called out of *ekklesia* can happen. The Revelation of the King Jesus becomes the foundation upon which the *ekklesia* are built, as they enforce the rule of the King at the city gates and cause that region to begin to look like the kingdom of Heaven. The *Ekklesia* is the legislative body of Christ, sent with keys of authority to cause the culture of heaven to manifest on earth until the kingdoms of this world become the kingdoms of our God. The kingdom cannot extend without the extension of kingdom culture that flows from *ekklesia* gatherings who have been shaped and equipped through intimate discipleship with the King. What is kingdom culture and how does that correlate with discipleship? Well I am glad you asked! Webster defines culture as:

A: "The customary beliefs, social forms, and material traits of a racial, religious, or social

52

group *also*: the characteristic features of everyday existence (such as diversions or a way of life) shared by people in a place or time. Example: popular *culture,* Southern *culture*

B: The set of shared attitudes, values, goals, and practices that characterizes an institution or organization. Example: a corporate *culture* focused on the bottom line

C: The set of values, conventions, or social practices associated with a particular field, activity, or societal characteristic studying the effect of computers on print *culture.* *Example:* Changing the *culture* of materialism will take time …— Peggy O'Mara

D: The integrated pattern of human knowledge, belief, and behavior that depends upon the capacity for learning and transmitting knowledge to succeeding generations.

2a: enlightenment and excellence of taste acquired by intellectual. Example: aesthetic training

B: acquaintance with and taste in fine arts, humanities, and broad aspects of science as distinguished from vocational and technical skills. Example: a person of *culture"*.

When we see this definition of culture and think in terms of kingdom culture, the importance of discipleship that leads to a mature *ekklesia* is essential if the body of Christ is to establish the culture of heaven on earth. The kingdom culture would include the customary beliefs, social forms, and the characteristic features of everyday way of the life of the kingdom of heaven. The values, goals, and practices that characterize the kingdom as found in the revelation of the teachings of Torah scriptures would be taught to the disciples as they walked with Jesus. The behavior and belief system of the Spirit of life, as opposed to the deadness, which comes from the letter of the law, would produce a transformed *ekklesia* that would be a legislative body to transform culture.

Jesus was training and equipping His disciples for apostolic conquest. David Francis Bacon explains it this way:

> "During the time of the ancient Greek orator Demosthenes (384-322 BC), the word apostolos was a naval term that described an admiral, the fleet of ships that traveled with him and the specialized crew who accompanied and assisted the admiral.
>
> The fleet would be sent out to sea on a mission to locate territories where civilization was nonexistent. Once an uncivilized region was identified, the admiral (called the *apostolos*)— along with his specialized crew and all their cargo and belongings—would disembark, settle down, and work as a team to establish a new community. Then they would begin the process of transforming a strange land into a replica of life as they believed it should be. Their purpose was total *colonization* of the uncivilized territory.
>
> Within this special fleet of ships were both the personnel and the cargo required to establish a new culture, a new life, and a new community. When that fleet pulled up to shore, it contained

workers trained to build roads, construct buildings, and teach uncivilized natives [sic] how to read, write, and function in a new kind of social order. Thus, the admiral became the team leader for the construction of a new society.

Once the job was completed, a majority of the team members reboarded the ships and launched out to sea again to find another uncivilized area and repeat the entire colonization process all over again. Thus, we find that the word *apostolos* described an admiral or team leader who led a team to establish new communities in uncivilized territories.[23]

When Jesus began to preach that the kingdom of heaven is at hand, repentance was needed because a shift in their way of life and culture was required in order to walk with Him, the long awaited Messiah, who would arrive with the keys of the kingdom to deliver them out of bondage and into the Lord's promises.

Kingdom Culture and Discipleship

What Jesus was inviting His disciples into what not just training in what He taught so that they could do what He did, but they were being invited into the culture and the way of the King. Their very allegiance to their own way of life and culture was being left behind as they joined themselves together to learn the culture and way of the kingdom of heaven. Culture

---

[23] David Francis Bacon, *Lives of the Apostles of Jesus Christ* (New Haven: L. H. Young, 1836), p. 8

includes the beliefs, customs, and arts of a particular society and their belief systems that have been cultivated over time. Culture can also be described as the personality of a society or group. Culture is a way of thinking, behaving, and living that is considered common, normal, or dominant within a certain group of people. Walking with God also means that we are daily living life with the King of glory and walking in His ways, and becoming a habitation of His Presence. Walking with God means we are walking with the King and learning the culture of the kingdom of heaven. As the disciples walked with Jesus, they learned about the kingdom protocols through seeing Jesus modeling them.

If discipleship with Jesus is also walking in the council of the Lord, then the *ekklesia* is the extension of the authority of Christ the King to administrate and legislate both justice and the judicial decisions made within His divine council. Discipleship is the preparation of walking in His divine council in order to move as a mature *ekklesia,* having the keys of knowledge necessary for administering the dictates of the law of the Spirit in regions on earth, functioning as an embassy of heaven on earth. This results in the ambassadors of Christ carrying word and ministry of reconciliation or the ministry of atonement, which cries, "be reconciled to God." Let the earth and nations, through the blood of Jesus, be reconciled back to their original design and intent.

The Potter's Wheel and the Birthing Stool of Reformation

The Body of Christ is on the cusp of a New Era as we enter into 2020 and there is a critical need for pioneers and forerunners to prepare the way. This preparation for the reformation of kingdom culture is necessary because we are about to walk a *way* corporately which we have not travelled before in this generation. It is one thing to have revival and restoration, but if the kingdom structure of reformation is going to happen, then it will be like pouring new wine into old wineskins, if we are not prepared beforehand. We cannot take what is being restored and put it into an individualist, humanistic culture that operates in both the world and the church, and still expect reformation. Restoration of the kingdom cannot be separated from the reformation and reinstitution of kingdom culture. Restoration is not about what we want in the kingdom, but it is about what the Father wants. In a kingdom culture, the King gets what He wants, for it is a theocratic kingdom and not a democracy.

With all that being said, there must be some uprooting and tearing down of kingdoms that do not align with the gospel of the kingdom before there can be building and planting of *ekklesia*. In the book of Jeremiah, God instructs Jeremiah to go down to the potter's house so He can reveal something to him:

> *1 The word that came to Jeremiah from the LORD, saying, 2 "Arise, and go down to the potter's house, and there I will cause thee to hear my words." 3 Then I went down to the potter's house, and, behold, he wrought a work on the wheels. 4 And the vessel that he made of clay was marred in the hand of the potter: so he made it again on another vessel, as seemed good to the potter to make it.*

Jeremiah 18:1-4

The potter was making a work on the wheel and this was a prophetic picture to Jeremiah regarding the

57

nation of Israel. The work in the hands of the potter is a clay vessel that sits positioned on the potter's wheel. As we've seen, the Hebrew word *melakah* means *work*, which derives from the same root as kingdom, messenger, and walk! The word *melakah* comes directly from the word *malak,* which means *angel, messenger, or ambassador.* So the work of clay on the potter's wheel is being shaped and formed into a vessel prepared to be an ambassador of the kingdom. The same language of Jeremiah 1:10, where the Lord declares that Jeremiah was a prophet to the nation to root out, pull down, destroy and tear down before the building and planting, can be compared to the shaping of the clay on the potter's wheel. That is, as we are being conformed into the image of Christ, He is uprooting, pulling down, destroying and tearing down every system and kingdom that has marred His image in us, in order to make us fit vessels to pour out glory.

The word for *wheel* is only used two places in the Old Testament, and that is here in Jeremiah and also in Exodus 1:16, where the midwives are assisting the Hebrew women give birth on the birthing stool. Even though this same Hebrew word is used in two different ways, I believe that prophetically it is showing us a picture. It is in the secret and intimate place of discipleship where the hand of God is forming us in the prophetic womb into the image of Christ. It is on the potter's wheel and the birthing stool that birth pains are experienced, as we are being prepared. The potter saw that the vessel was marred so he reworked it and put it back on the wheel. The Lord is cleaning and reforming vessels on the potter's wheel, and it is through walking with Jesus that we become transformed into His image through allowing His hands to shape us into His image.

The Workmanship of God and Dispatching of Messengers

*8 For by grace you have been saved through faith, and that not of yourselves; it is the gift of God, 9 not of works, lest anyone should boast. 10 For we are His **workmanship,** created in Christ Jesus **for good works,** which God prepared beforehand that we should walk in them.*

Ephesians 2:8-10

Let us revisit the Hebrew definition for walk and kingdom before I begin to unfold the powerful correlation to workmanship. Recall that the Hebrew word *melakah* 'work' is '"' shares the same root as *halak* 'walk' and *malak* 'kingdom,' and can be interpreted as, *a message through action.* *Melakah* is used in Genesis 2:2 when the Scripture says that God ended His work. *Melakah* also translates as *workmanship, deputyship, or ministry.* It derives from *malak*, which means *to dispatch as a deputy or messenger, or to be an ambassador or an angel.* God rested from forming His workmanship, so that His work could be done through His creation.

Therefore, what is the point of all of this and how does it connect to walk? Well I am glad that you asked! In the Jeremiah 18, the potter was producing a *work* on the *wheel.* The same word for *work* in Jeremiah is *melakah* thus, as we *walk* with God, we are being shaped, pressed, and formed into a messenger or ambassador of the kingdom and are dispatched into our assignment. Through our *walk* we are birthed and dispatched out of the place of intimacy, so that we might produce the *works* of God. We walk by faith to produce the works of God. In simple terms, producing the work and action of the messenger means being a doer of the word and not just a hearer only (James 1:23).

Faith and Works

Faith apart from works is an incomplete revelation. Faith is the substance of things hoped for and evidence of unseen realms (Hebrews 11:1). The word *faith* in Greek is *hupostasis* which means 'the underlying state or underlying substance or essence, which is the fundamental reality that supports all else.' Literally, it means 'to set under support.' It can also be used to mean 'confidence, trust, foundation, or what has actual existence.'

Hupostasis is also the word Greeks used for a title deed, which is why the Amplified translation uses the phrase *title deed* instead of *substance*. Faith occurs when our encounter with the reality of the existence of the Godhead creates in us an entire new foundation and confidence, which we live by. When Paul states we walk by faith and not by sight (2 Corinthians 5:7), it does not mean we walk blindly, but rather that we see with the eyes of the Spirit. When the illumination of the Spirit comes, the eyes of our heart are flooded with light and the chaos of darkness and the refuse of lies are washed away through that revelation of Jesus Christ. It is the light of Christ that sets parameters and order in our walk, for *His word is a lamp for our feet and light on our path* (Psalms 119:105).

As great as the revelatory dimension of faith and encountering Christ is, it is incomplete apart from works. Two aspects of works that must be understood in order to catch that revelation are found in the letter from James the Apostle to the church:

*17 Thus also **faith** by itself, if it does not have **works,** is **dead**. 18 But someone will say, "You have **faith**, and I have works." Show me your faith without your works, and I will **show** you my **faith by my works**.*

James 1:17-18

*21 Was not Abraham our father **justified by works** when he offered Isaac his son on the altar? 22 Do you see that faith was **working together with his works**, and by works faith was made perfect?*

James 2:21-22

James is clearly saying that by doing works one's faith is shown, and that Abraham was justified in that manner. Yet it seems to contradict other scriptures about Abraham with regard to faith and works:

*8 For by grace you have been saved through faith, and that not of yourselves; it is the gift of God, 9 **not of works**, lest anyone should boast.*

Ephesians 2:8-9

*2 For if Abraham was **justified by works**, he has something to boast about, but not before God. 3 For what does the Scripture say? "Abraham believed God, and it was accounted to him for righteousness." 4 Now to him who works, the **wages** are not counted as **grace** but as **debt**. 5 But to him who **does not work** but believes on Him who justifies the ungodly, his faith is accounted for righteousness.*

Romans 4:2-5

Let's compare the Greek and Hebrew words for *works* to investigate further. The Greek word for *work* in James is *ergon*, which means '*a business, employment, or **anything that has been produced or a***

61

product.' This is also the word used in Romans and Ephesians. So we can conclude that the work is the product that has been produced, not just something we do from a Hebrew way of thought. The Pharisees asked Jesus how they could produce the works of God, and His response was quite interesting;

> *28 Then they said to Him, "What shall we do, that we may **work the works of God**?" 29 Jesus answered and said to them, "This is the **work of God**, that you **believe** in Him whom He sent."*
>
> John 6:28-29

The work of God is to believe in Him whom He sent! Abraham believed God and the DNA of God was *produced* in Abraham and he became righteous. The evidence that Abraham had faith was in his actions and works, that is, the life that was a product of his faith:

> *21 Was not Abraham our father justified by works when he offered Isaac his son on the altar? 22 Do you see that faith was working together with his works, and by works faith was made perfect? 23 And the Scripture was fulfilled which says, "Abraham believed God, and it was accounted to him for righteousness." And he was called the friend of God. 24 You see then that a man is **justified by works, and not by faith only**.*
>
> James 2:21-24

It is important to understand that the works of God produced out of walking with God in discipleship, is not works of the flesh, but the works of the Spirit:

*1 Thus the heavens and the earth, and all the host of them, were finished. 2 And on the seventh day God ended His **work** which He had done, and He rested on the seventh day from all His **work**, which He had done.*

Genesis 2:1-2

*1 The heavens declare the glory of God; and the firmament shows His **handiwork**.*

Psalms 19:1

The *action or work* of our walk is our lifestyle. The work is the fruit that is produced in our walk as we live out the message. Then, while we are walking out the message of the kingdom, God is creating or producing His nature in us. Just as the heavens and the firmament declare the glory of God and show his handiwork, we are meant to display the work of God to principalities and powers through a *corporate* lifestyle of the kingdom as we learn to abide in Him *individually.*

Chapter 7
Fathers Casting Vision for Discipleship

Throughout the journey of this book, I have focused mainly on the intimate discipleship aspect of walking with God, which is of the utmost importance. He alone is our Savior, Bridegroom, Master, and King. With that being said, we cannot effectively address discipleship without the inclusion the fathers and mothers who are sent to prepare sons and daughters to be part of a mature legislative and governmental body of believers, carrying out the commandments of Jesus. Spiritual fathers and sons walking together has Biblical precedence in the Old Testament with relationships like Moses and Joshua or Elijah and Elisha. We also have some New Testament models of this relationship such as John the Baptist and his disciples, Paul and Timothy, and of course Jesus and the disciples. Jesus' declaration to His disciples that, "Upon this rock I will build My *ekklesia*," is not for an institution called *church*, but a family of inheritors called an *ekklesia*.

Fathers and Sons: Walking in Inheritance

The coming of Jesus, the Apostle and High Priest of our faith, is the direct result of the love of the Father. "For God so loved the world that He sent…" the only ambassador who could fully represent Him and bring reconciliation--His Son. This is not to say that Jesus is not fully God and therefore inferior to the Father, but rather that His function as a son is to express the nature of The Father, for sons express the nature of their father. For example, the Hebrew word *banah* means build, is which originates from the root *ben,* the Hebrew word for *son.* The profound truth of the root word *to build* gives illumination to the concept of *building.* The root contains the two letters *bet* 'house' and *nun* 'seed' or 'continue.' Together this word means, "*continue the house.* In this context, the house can be a literal building or tent, or figuratively, a household with sons who carry the DNA of their father and continue the legacy of the house.[24]

Psalms 127:1 declares, "Unless the Lord builds the house they labor in vain." Yet verses three and four go on to say that children are an inheritance, fruit of the womb, and arrows in the hand of a mighty man. This speaks of much more than a literal building of an edifice. (However, this is in no way and excuse not to attend one either.) Rather, it speaks of the continuing of inheritance.

If building is related to sons (and by implication, daughters), then fathers and mothers of the faith have a direct part to play in bringing children of the faith into maturity. The kingdom is about inheritance and if the inheritance of believers are the nations, then sons and daughters must be equipped and trained to step into their inheritance. When Elijah was about to be caught up with the Lord, Elisha asked him for a double portion. Elisha was not asking to do twice as many miracles as Elijah, but it was the request to be a first born son who would continue the work of his father (Deuteronomy 21:17).

Fathers and Mothers Casting Vision

---

[24] Jeff Benner. *Ancient Hebrew Lexicon Bible Dictionary*

Discipline your son, and he will give you rest;
he will give delight to your heart. Where there
is no prophetic vision the people cast off
restraint, but blessed is he who keeps the law.

Proverbs 29:18

Parents in discipleship cast prophetic vision of the divine destiny of children in the faith to be conformed to the image of Jesus by setting daily parameters for how they are to walk until reach the maturity level necessary to carry the responsibility of inheritance. Fathers cast vision for the path that sons might walk in to accomplish their God given assignment from the heavenly Father. True fathers and mothers cast vision out of the blueprints they have received from walking in the council of the Lord. Sons and daughters, who have been assigned to them, possess an inheritance in some measure from the same blueprint. It is their inheritance. But the beauty of discipleship is to equip sons and daughters to walk in it with integrity and honor, yet at the same time to move for the heavenly Father in the uniqueness of their design. Discipling parents do not produce carbon copies or puppets, but authentic, mature sons and daughters.

My Journey as a Son

In my walk with the Lord, I had spiritual fathers and mothers assigned to me, because at that stage in my maturity we carried similar assignments. They were His hands and feet, co-laboring with Him, shaping different aspects of my character in order to enable me to handle the weight of my assignment in that given season. I was God's field and His building as He co-labored with fathers and mothers to plant and build within me a place for His habitation. Walking with fathers and mothers

67

gave context to the blueprints the Heavenly Father was revealing to me. They were able to give practical application and bring articulation to what I did not have the spiritual understanding and wisdom to fully comprehend and articulate. Through these relationships, I was able to take what was existing in the Spirit and see it manifest in my daily walk in every area of influence.

True spiritual fathers will always tell you the truth because they are not impressed with your gifting, because they are more concerned about your character and your ability to walk in purpose. They carry an inheritance that will break the limits off sons who submit to the process necessary for that to happen.

Fathers show sons the blueprint, which will bring tribulation. Tribulation comes because they have now become pregnant with purpose. The tribulation that purpose brings will cause sons to feel confined within the parameters of their purpose while God is forming Christ in them. Yet those same parameters will eventually become the place of their greatest freedom. Fathers are concerned about true liberty. True liberty is to be who you are created to be in Christ.

The Process: From Confirming to Conforming

This process of walking with God aligned with spiritual fathers and mothers happened in the midst of the call and the commission of various aspects of the blueprints I was shown by the Father. As the Father cast vision to me directly, he also sent fathers and mothers not only to *confirm* it, but also co-labor with God to see me *conformed* to it. This conforming was not to make me who they were, but instead my conforming to the design the Father had for me which they received by divine insight. Every scope from each of them was different, but all spoke into the blueprint for my life. Some of the best fathering I received was not just sitting down and hearing revelation, but doing life with them and hearing insights that they would never share from behind a pulpit. The vision for me as a son may have been clear, but fathers gave context to the process and the wilderness experience. It helped me to understanding that chastisement and scourging from the Father was a mark of my sonship.

Some Lessons I Have Learned

Throughout my 20-year journey with the Lord, I have experienced rejection more times, than I can count. Some of it came because of moving in zeal without wisdom. Some was the result of believing the hype from others and moving in rebellion as a son, instead of enjoying the peace of obscurity. Other times rejection came from things like unhealthy fathering, betrayal, being misunderstood, or just simply deception in my own mind. Nevertheless, through it all, the point is that I have learned valuable lessons in every situation. I learned how valuable repentance and forgiveness are. I learned how precious wisdom is that comes out of the healing of wounds after humiliation and rejection. I have learned the value of process. I learned how to show honor someone, even when I do not agree with them, as well as how to move in honor, even when I am being wronged.

I have been a rebellious son who was healed and I have been a loyal son who was wounded, yet never dishonored. In all, I have learned the importance of fathering, as well as the importance of being a loyal son. I also learned it is better to be transparent as opposed to involuntary exposure. Either way, pride must be broken. These are a few things I have learned in a lifelong journey of learning as a son.

Chapter 8
Enoch and the Ascending and Descending Life of Discipleship

22 Enoch walked with God after he fathered Methuselah 300 years and had other sons and daughters. 23 Thus, all the days of Enoch were 365 years. 24 Enoch walked with God, and he was not, for God took him.

Genesis 5:22-24

In my years of walking with the Lord in intimacy and discipleship, there were many occasions that I received profound wisdom and revelation in the secret place of prayer. I came to understand that those times of intimacy and unveiling of revelation were meant to be walked out in every day practical living. This is what I will refer to as: The Ascending and Descending Walk of Discipleship. That is, one metaphorically ascends to a heavenly place of intimacy with the Lord, and then descends back to earth, so to speak, where one then walks out what has been learned in intimacy while back in community with others.

Enoch walked with God for three hundred years, so his being caught up in fellowship with the Lord could very well have been continuous, until God finally kept him with Him, or as the scriptures say, 'took him.' It is interesting to note that in the Septuagint or Greek translation of this passage, *walked with God* is translated *pleased God,* which explains the significance of Hebrews 11:5:

5 By faith, Enoch was taken up so that he should not see death, and he was not found, because God had taken him. Now before he was taken he was commended as having pleased God.

Hebrews 11:5

Enoch pleased God because he walked with Him in intimacy and obedience. Enoch *was not* because *he was not found*. He was not found because God took Him and kept Him. The ascending aspect of intimate discipleship is when we begin to dwell in the secret place with the Lord, where He reveals and unveils the beauty of His nature. Paul declares that, "We are seated with Him in heavenly places," (Ephesians 2:6). Since, according to the Psalmist, Christ is seated at the right hand of the Father, then we are seated with Him there until He makes His enemies His footstool:

The LORD says to my Lord: "Sit at my right hand, until I make your enemies your footstool."

Psalms 110:1

The Hebrew word *yashab* 'sit' means, *to abide, to dwell, to marry, to tarry, to habitate.*[25] *Yashab* derives from the root *shub*, which means *to sit in a seat and rest*, and is the same root as *Sabbath* 'rest.' The idea of *sitting* indicates a place of learning, not for Christ, but for His Bride, His body, His *Ecclesia*. Sitting is a position of learning until we understand how to make our enemies our footstool. The ascending aspect of discipleship is learning the reality of the blessings that were poured out through Christ's death, burial, and resurrection, until we shift from merely knowing our position in Him to actively manifesting the fruit of it in maturity. The seat of Christ or being seated at Christ's feet is where we learn how to actively walk

---

[25] Strong's Lexicon Exhaustive Concordance.

out the message of the kingdom, how to stand in the midst of attack, and how to let the fruit of that message *descend* into every sphere of our life. It is in this sitting before him that we learn to trust Him in all our ways, and not just the ways everyone sees!

Through living an ascended lifestyle of abiding in Him, we descend and begin to walk out that message in daily living, as we become transformed by that message and produce the fruit of it. The abiding place of being seated with Him is where we become one with Him in our ways. Paul proclaims that we should "not be conformed to this world, but transformed by the renewing of our minds that we may prove (be the proof) of His good, acceptable, and perfect will" (Romans 12:1). Verse 2 is inherently connected to verse 1, and it says that we are to "offer our bodies as a living sacrifice holy and acceptable to God that is our act of worship." The place of ascending is the place of intimacy where we dwell with God who is an all-consuming fire and the place of descending is manifesting Christ in our daily lives, as witnesses of His resurrection. In the following sections, I give some practical examples, along with some experiences, to convey what I mean by the ascending and descending of discipleship.

When Revelation Becomes an Idol

I once had an interesting vision that taught me a lot about the importance of walking out the revelations we receive and not treating them as trophies. It happened in two stages over a period of a few years. In 2007, I awoke up one morning and suddenly I entered into "an encounter." I was in a room that seemed to be a waiting room. There were others there as well, but we were all waiting for different things from God. Suddenly, a huge ball of light entered, and out of it came this huge angel. This angel was dressed like a chauffeur, so I knew I was about to go on a journey! He appeared with a very serious look on his face, even a little perturbed maybe, pointed to me, and then pointed to the wall. As I looked at the wall, an invisible door appeared. Yet I could see it and somehow I knew that I was supposed to go through it. The excitement that I had felt was like "this is what I have been waiting for!" As I stepped into the door, first with just my right foot, I could see gold and furniture that was so bright it was hard to look at. So I thought this has to be the throne room! When I stepped through with my other foot and came all the way through the door, I stepped back into my bedroom and the encounter was over!

I thought to myself, "What just happened?" It was not until a few years later, after inquiring of the Lord about the meaning of the encounter that I was once again brought back into this place in a vision. I stepped back into the gold-filled room and it was some kind of treasury room. There were different types of vessels inscribed with titles of teachings I had taught before! I then understood that I had accumulated revelations, yet I was not fully walking them out in my personal walk! (The point of the encounter, I believe, was not whether there is a literal place in the spirit called "my personal treasury room," but rather that this was the language of the Spirit. Therefore, I am not building a doctrine here, but only sharing an encounter).

I was being shown that I valued receiving and preaching revelation more than I valued fully walking it out personally! When this was revealed to me, I knew that I must fully walk out this truth in order to be prepared for the days ahead. So I did not minister anywhere for two years after this and I just went into a kind of ministry hiding, worked a job, spent time with my family, and spent intense time in the secret place with the Lord. This was the worst and the best two years of my life! God deconstructed me, then rebuilt, reformed, and revived me in ways I did not know I needed. A significant truth that came to me in this season was that I needed the spirit of wisdom in order to properly operate with revelation, because that way Christ could be revealed in me, making what I preached a testimony of my walk.

There is much more to this story, but my point is that I wanted to be transparent and convey my heart in sharing it. My desire is to keep young ministers who have fallen in love with revelation from wrecking households because they fail to walk out their revelations or to manifest the nature of Messiah. . When the testing of the word comes, if we have not gone through the process of walking it out, our failure will affect us, as well as those assigned to us. The revelation itself had become an idol to me. But now, I no longer care about platforms or the desire to share all the revelation I receive. What I care about is that the revelations of Jesus be manifest in my life, first as a husband, father, son, friend, etc. I now realize that the reason the angel came dressed as a driver was to take me on a journey of walking out revelation through wisdom, so I would become what had been revealed.

A significant amount of transformation happened in my life through the two years I sat down. I did not do it because of sin in my life, but I needed it in order to walk in what was given to me. Everyone that I mentor, disciple or father knows that some of the first questions I ask them is, "What is your prayer life like and what do your wife and kids say about how you act when no one sees you?"

I have seen this trap happen time and again while leading, training, and equipping people. There is a danger of people falling in love with being on the platform and having an accumulation of revelation, without any intention of seeing it transform their own characters.

Prophetic Process: Walking Out the Message

From this encounter, I began to understand the importance of walking out not only every revelation I received, but also every true prophetic word from the Lord. Being a prophetic voice and one who has discipled prophetic people, the Achilles heel of many prophetic people is not walking out prophetic words they have received and given through intimacy and discipleship in their own lives. There are several examples in Scripture that display the importance of prophetic process.

Joseph: From Dreams to Reality

Joseph is one example of prophetic process. Joseph has a dream where he sees prophetically that he will rule over his family, but what he does not see is the process required to bring that dream to reality (Genesis 37:5-11). I love how the Psalmist describes the process of Joseph from the dream to the fulfillment:

> *He had sent a man ahead of them, Joseph, who was sold as a slave. ¹⁸ His feet were hurt with fetters; his neck was put in a collar of iron; ¹⁹ until what he had said came to pass, the word of the LORD tested him.*
>
> Psalms 105:17-19

Scripture says that God sent Joseph ahead to be catalyst for Israel! The word tested Joseph until he was prepared to fulfill the reason for the dream. The process between the dream and reality according to Scripture was the word of the Lord came to test Joseph. The Hebrew word *tsaraph* 'test' means, "To fuse (metal); that is, to refine, refiner founder, goldsmith, melt, purify, purge, or to try." It is the same the word used in Malachi 3 when the prophet speaks of the Lord coming as a refiner's fire and fuller's soap (Zechariah 3:2-3). A fuller was the person who used a harsh soap on sheep's wool in order to get it clean and prepared to be used. Isaiah used the same word *tsaraph* to describe the Lord purging away the dross as He rids Himself of His enemies and adversaries. The word *tsaraph* also comes from the word that means 'crucible,' which is a pot used for melting metals that will be poured into a mold. *Crucible* also means intense and severe trial, in which the interaction brings about a transformation, as in the sentence, "His character was forged in the crucible of war" (Webster's Dictionary). Joseph was being refined and forged to become a deliverer through intense trial by the very word of prophecy sent to him in his dreams.

Psalms 105:17 declares that God sent Joseph to Egypt to fulfill His covenantal purposes to promised through Abraham, Isaac, and Jacob. The word of the Lord comes first to the *deliverer* to deliver and prepare them to be the Lord's vessels of deliverance to others. Joseph was a deliverer, being melted, purged, and refined within the crucible of the word he received, so that he could be sent to bring deliverance and promise to a nation not yet fully formed. He had to be melted, purged, and refined in order to be able to be poured into the image and mold of God's deliverer. The word *disciplined* him referred to placing affliction on his feet (or his *walk*) through fetters and putting a collar of iron on his neck. The word *tsaraph* was also used to describe the Messiah coming into the temple to purify the sons of Levi, as mentioned above (Malachi 3:1), which gives us a profound truth in walking with God.

The dimension of our walk with God shifts when the revelation of Jesus Christ comes to us in different seasons. In a sense, an aspect of walking with God is being a disciple of the very word that comes to us, whether through prophetic word or revelation of Scripture. Jesus "the Word" comes to unveil Himself in ways we have not seen previously, which brings with it the refining, purging, and discipline needed to prepare us to be His image bearers. The word is the refiner and crucible that prepares us to walk in the *mold* of His image and to become witnesses of the Resurrection and ambassadors of the King. It took Joseph 13 years to walk out the revelation of his dream. He was tested from the pit, shunned by his family, falsely accused while at Potiphar's house, and ultimately forgotten in prison. Through the testing, Joseph passed the test and increased in favor because He walked with God and was disciplined in every way to carry the wisdom and understanding necessary to fulfill a destiny that far outstretched his imagination.

David: From Anointed in Secret to King

The melting pot of reformation is where the reformer becomes transformed and reformed into a forerunner—a preview of the coming attraction. The coming attraction is an army of deliverers and reformers who have passed the test and are poised to see regional, national and international reformation. This reformation will melt away of the dross of mere religion that produces form without power and instead birth a generation that walks in the image of the greatest reformer who ever lived—a Jesus Christ.

Another illustration of walking out a message to become that message is the story of King David.

13 Then Samuel took the horn of oil and anointed him in the midst of his brothers. And the Spirit of the Lord rushed upon David from that day forward.

1 Samuel 16:13

David, the eighth son of Jesse, was not invited to the anointing service of the next king! Even though the Scripture says that David was anointed that day and the Spirit of the Lord was upon him in secret, he had not yet been prepared to walk in the very purpose of his calling. He was anointed King of Israel, yet King Saul, whom the Lord rejected, was still reigning as king. Though David was both called and anointed to be king, he did not become king until he was processed by walking out what the reality of being king encompassed. David was anointed to be king, but at the time, he was a shepherd. Though there are characteristics of shepherding that would help him as king, David still had to learn what it meant to be a king of Yahweh. Each test that David passed, from killing the lion and the bear, to taking out Goliath, and overcoming the attacks of Saul were all part of the process of walking out the message of the king in order to become one in character and fruit, and not just in name.

There were many kings throughout the time of Israel, but very few walked in the ways of David. It is one thing to be called a prophet, apostle or any other leadership title, and yet another thing to walk in the function of it. The time between the calling and commissioning of David was fifteen years. While Josephus the historian says David was ten years old, most scholars place David at around age 15 when he

79

was called. That would make him around thirty years old when he became King of Judah. But it was not until seven years later that he became king over all of Israel, which makes the time until the full kingship longer than fifteen years.

In light of that, one of the greatest gifts the Lord has given to me is an awareness of process. There have been many times in my twenty-one years of walking with God that I thought I was ready to walk in my calling and the Lord said no. Waiting has cultivated so much in my heart that I now understand the value of process. That process comes step by step through discipleship and has the result of removing the biggest enemy to a healthy and mature commissioning—the image we see in the mirror.

Encountering the Burning One

When the revelation of Jesus Christ comes to us, we begin to encounter the burning man who sits upon the throne. He is the refiner who comes into His temple (us) and burns away anything that is not like Him. He is an all-consuming fire and a jealous God (Deuteronomy 4:24). When the Burning One comes, He does not just come to simply encounter us and leave, but his coming begins a new aspect of walking with him and a refining fire which accomplish what He is after.

In 2005, while I still relatively young in ministry, I had an encounter with the Lord that forever changed me. At the time, I was already moving in the things of God, ordained, and preaching the gospel. Prior to this encounter, for about a year or so, I was experiencing dreams and visions from God at least three nights a week. I thought the Lord was really pouring out revelation to me until one day, as I woke up in the morning, suddenly, I was taken to a place in the spirit.

In this encounter, I found myself in an ancient temple. As I walked through the corridor, suddenly I went through a door and was in a secret chamber or council room. This was the largest room I had ever seen, and in this room I saw the Being–who-was-engulfed-in fire sitting on the throne conducting council with a remnant of people there. The fear that I felt when I entered the room was so great that I just knew I had entered Hell and this was Satan himself!

As I attempted to sneak out the room, the door was locked! That room was ancient, and every step I took made a sound. So when I tried to get out of the room, this Being-of-fire, the Burning Man, heard me. He stopped his council and turned his attention towards me. To say I was gripped with fear would be an understatement! When this being looked at me, a river of fire came from his mouth and it was moving toward me. I started pulling on the door with everything I had and crying out to God, "What did I do and why am I in Hell?"

All of a sudden, the fire coming from his mouth engulfed me, and instantly I was back in my room. Then I could hear two audible voices, yet I could not understand their language.

After this encounter, as I submitted it to a spiritual father and sought the Lord, I realized that I had not been in Hell, but I had been in the presence of His glory! This encounter was so far from my grid of understanding, that the only thing I could equate it with was Hell, so it must have been the devil! The fear I experienced could not be described with words.

I had a real encounter with Jesus the Burning One, and He destroyed *my limited image of Him!* The most wonderful result of this encounter was that once the language of fire engulfed me, I began to have revelation of scripture unlike I ever had before. It was like the experience in the book of Daniel:

> *9 I watched till thrones were put in place, and the Ancient of Days was seated; his garment was white as snow, and the hair of His head was like pure wool. His throne was a fiery flame, its wheels a burning fire; 10 A fiery stream issued and came forth from before Him. A thousand thousands ministered to Him; ten thousand times ten thousand stood before Him. The court was seated, and the **books were opened.***

Daniel 7:9-10

My walk with God and the intimacy I experienced as a result of that encounter began to become intense, as He burned out religious forms and systems in me in preparation for me to disciple those who burned with fire for revival and reformation, just as I did. The ascending of encounters and experience will never reach their full potential if we do not walk out those revelations in discipleship and intimacy with the Lord. If we only ascend without descending, we have missed the authority to bring change because we are changed.

Walking Worthy of Your Calling

In the beginning of Chapter 4 of Ephesians, Paul urges the believers, as follows:

> *1 I therefore, a prisoner for the Lord, urge you to walk in a manner worthy of the calling to which you have been called, 2 with all humility and gentleness, with patience, bearing with one another in love, 3 eager to maintain the unity of the Spirit in the bond of peace.*

Paul admonishes the Ephesians to live a lifestyle that displays and brings value to the divine calling of becoming like Christ. In our being seated with Christ in heavenly places, we are learning how to put our enemies under our feet so that we know how to stand strong and walk out what we learn, until the fruit of His life is seen. Our life was meant to display the light of the glory of the Lord as we produce the fruit of humility, meekness, and patience, bearing with one another in love. The value we put on the gift of salvation we have called to and the grace we have received will be seen in our daily walk. We have been given the divine invitation to walk in union with Jesus, to walk as He walked, and to carry out the mandate of the kingdom to cause earth to look like heaven. The fruit of the life of Christ appearing in our daily walk as we mature is a sign and beacon in the midst of a dark world.

The light of the gospel will be seen to be increasing in the midst of a humanity in the midst of darkness. Walking worthy of the calling can be likened to the twelve spies who spied out the promise land and came back with fruit on their shoulders, proclaiming, "We are well able to overcome the giants in our land of promise." It was not miracles, signs, and wonders, that showed they were well able to overcome the giants that occupied their land of promise, but the fruit on their shoulders was the proof! It was proof that God was telling the truth about the land and that the land was indeed flowing with milk and honey. Prophetically speaking, the proof of the reality of the victory of Christ to bring us out of out a spiritual Egypt and into a promised land is seen in the fruit demonstrated by those have tasted of the good word and the power of the age to come (Hebrews 6:5). Those who have tasted of the good word are those who have been initiated into communion with the body and the blood of Christ to have daily communion with Him, as John declares:

> *7 But if we walk in the light, as he is in the light, we have fellowship with one another, and the blood of Jesus his Son cleanses us from all sin.*
>
> 1 John 1:7

Walk in the Light

As we walk in the light of the gospel, what we have been given through Christ Jesus in His death, burial, resurrection, and ascension is illuminated for us. When we walk in the light as John describes, the revelation of the blood of Jesus begins to cleanse us and washes away our sins. *Walking* denotes stepping into the realities of the kingdom, not just reading it from a positional stance. It is one thing to know that the blood of Jesus washes away our sins as a believer, yet it is another thing entirely to walk in the reality of the sanctifying power of His blood, as our soul and conscience become free from past bondages and sin.

John declares that God just does not shine light…He is light (1 John 1:5). If we compare this to John's gospel, the Word (Jesus) is that light and that light is the life of all men (John 1:4-5). In the gospel of John, Jesus, the Word Incarnate, is the light and life of all men that come into the world. If the word is the expression of thought and light is the illumination of what was hidden, this is why Paul says that Christ has preeminence through his being the image of the invisible God (Colossians 1:15). When the revelation of Jesus' Word comes alive through intimately walking with Him, He becomes *incarnate* or *embodied* in our everyday life.

Listen to how John describes encountering the Word of life:

That which was from the beginning, which we have heard, which we have seen with our eyes, which we looked upon and have touched with our hands, concerning the word of life.

1 John 1:1-2

John is describing the tangibility of walking with Jesus, the Incarnate Word, how he seen Him with eyes, and touched Him with his hands. In Hebrew culture of interpretation, this physical seeing and touching is considered to be *concrete,* as compared to something being *abstract. Concrete* means to experience the world through your , or simply put the word that shows a definite change in character and action. John's literal explanation of encountering the Word of Life is also a prophetic picture of what transpires when we encounter Him, as well. Walking with the Word of Life brings constant illumination to our path, so we do not stumble over the very One who is supposed to be our foundation and cornerstone (Isaiah 8:14). His life is the lamp unto our feet and the light unto our pathway (Psalm 119:105), because Jesus not only laid the blueprint for sonship, but He also equips us in word and deed about how to walk in His ways.

The striking language found in the opening of both the epistle of 1 John and the gospel of John stems from them both start from the Beginning. It is in the midst of darkness and chaos that light brings order. One of the Hebrew roots for light means *order,* thus the illumination that comes from us walking in *the Light* serves to direct our path in the midst of darkness. Not only does John describe encountering the word of life, but he and the other disciples saw Him and bear witness of that life. John the apostle writes that Jesus was the witness of the Father and now they bear witness of the Son, so that ultimately we all may be brought into that same fellowship with the Father and the Son. Walking in the light also means we are walking in fellowship with the Godhead as He abides in us and we abide in Him.

Chapter 9
Enoch and The Bride:
Walking In Preparation for the
Bridegroom

One of the most profound typologies pertaining to Enoch walking with God is the picture of the Bride walking with Christ. In the context of the life of Enoch, the picture of the two oxen yoked together can be seen as the God of Israel being the older ox and Israel being the younger ox, and also the marriage covenant as it is expressed in Deuteronomy 28. In that chapter, the Lord sets the stage for the blessings or curses that come through obedience or disobedience, respectively. The first 15 verses are the blessings that come if you obey the covenant by walking in obedience to His commandments or the marriage contract and curses if you do not obey. There are several references in Scripture to God being a husband to Israel:

32 not like the covenant that I made with their fathers on the day when I took them by the hand to bring them out of the land of Egypt, my covenant that they broke, though I was their husband, declares the LORD.

Jeremiah 31:32

In the New Testament, we also see the church, the New Jerusalem, is referred to as being prepared for her husband:

2 And I saw the holy city, the New Jerusalem, coming down out of heaven from God, prepared as a bride adorned for her husband.

The relationship between God and His people is seen as a marriage and as a covenant that is based on intimacy. It is in the place of intimacy that we walk daily with the Bridegroom and learn to serve Him and obey— not out of obligation, but out of love. How can two walk together unless they agree (Amos 3:3)? The Hebrew word *ya'ad* 'agree' , means to meet by appointment or to betroth. The betrothal in Hebrew culture was the first part of the marriage and it can loosely be compared to an engagement to marry, though the betrothal is a much stronger covenant. For example, when Mary the mother of Jesus was betrothed to Joseph and was found with a child, Joseph would have to divorce her to cancel the wedding, and doing so would involve both families. Compare this to someone in our culture who is engaged being able to cancel the wedding by just independently calling it off or breaking up with the fiancé(e). Betrothal is when the marriage has not yet been consummated because the bridegroom has not come to live with the bride. Walking with Jesus is the beginning of a betrothal, as we begin to prepare ourselves for the Bridegroom's return to come and live with us.

The ultimate fulfillment of the Bridegroom coming for His Bride is the Second Coming of Jesus, but before He comes *for* us He is coming *to* us, as well as *through* us. The Bride must make herself ready by walking in the intimacy of discipleship. This is how the Bride makes herself ready to become the Wife (Revelation 19:7). Walking with Jesus teaches us how to love what He loves, hate what He hates, and to burn with zeal for what He burns with.

The First Adam and His Wife versus the Last Adam and His Wife

21 So the Lord God caused a deep sleep to fall upon the man, and while he slept took one of his ribs and closed up its place with flesh.22 And the rib that the Lord God had taken from the man he made into a woman and brought her to the man. 23 Then the man said, "This at last is bone of my bones   and flesh of my flesh; she shall be called Woman, because she was taken out of Man." 24 Therefore a man shall leave his father and his mother and hold fast to his wife, and they shall become one flesh. 25 And the man and his wife were both naked and were not ashamed.

Genesis 2:21-25

When God created woman, He described her as being bone of his bone and flesh of his flesh, meaning they were of the same species and there was a unique union between them. Genesis describes the woman as being a helpmeet to man, which interpreted means she would "declare, explain, and reveal the hidden glory along with her husband" (Genesis 2:18). Essentially Woman would be the proverbial "womb" of man, declaring the image of God, yet with a different and unique expression. Paul declares to the Corinthians that man is the glory of God, yet woman is the glory of man (1 Corinthians 11:9). If we take this typology and place it next to Last Adam, Jesus, and His Bride, the *Ekklesia*, we will see that the Bride is to express the glory of her husband in a way that can only be achieved through intimacy.

It is through walking in continually intimacy and union that the Bride begins to know the secrets of the heart of the Bridegroom. My beautiful wife Jeanette and I have been married for almost fifteen years. We have been together though for almost twenty-two years, so I have learned incredible lessons in our walk together as a couple that parallel many things in our relationship with the Bridegroom. When Jeanette and I first started dating, I would call her or she would call me. Either way, we had to learn to recognize each other's voice. The more we talked on the phone and spent time getting to know each other, the easier it was for me to recognize her voice. Through the years of cultivating intimacy and love, not only do we know each other's voices, but also now oftentimes we each know what the other one is thinking. This did not happen though osmosis or merely spending time together, but through active participation in knowing each other on a deep level.

We have learned each other's love language, which is extremely important. It will save you time and money! I used to think if I always bought her flowers, she would think I was the greatest husband in the world and she would shout it from the rooftop! I started to notice after many purchases of flowers that she did not care for flowers all the time. She loved the dishes being done or putting the kids to bed, so we could spend time together. I learned quickly though that this was her love language! (As a side note, she does like when I have flowers delivered to her job "just because"☺).

The point is that even though we loved each other we thought differently because our families grew up very different. When we left our parents' homes, we also left the different cultures that we were raised in, as well. Our journey in marriage was about establishing our own family culture that will look different from that of our respective upbringings. Our corporate journey as the Bride of Christ means leaving the culture of the world, clinging to the Bridegroom, and learning His culture. It is through this intimacy and discipleship that we begin to express the glory, the weight and the character of the Bridegroom. My wife and I went from learning each other's voice to learning each other's ways. Now she knows what I will say in many situations, because she knows my ways. I know how to please her because of knowing her ways, and her love language.

As we learn the ways of Jesus, we will understand His love language. God is an all-consuming fire and He is a jealous God (Deuteronomy 4:24). The Hebrew word for *consuming* and *eat* are the same, because fire consumes and we consume what we eat. In this truth lies Bridegroom's love language. He is jealous for His Bride and He will consume anything that separates us from Him. He also wants a Bride who is fully consumed with Him and who desires to commune with Him continually, by eating of His flesh and drinking of His blood. Prophetically speaking, the Bride who is consumed by what she consumes, which is the body and blood of Jesus. When Jesus declared this to the crowd, many left Him that day because they could not grasp the spiritual application (John 6:56). He declared, "My words are spirit and they are life" (John 6:63). As we walk with Jesus as His Bride, we are coming into union *with* Him and *in* Him, to the point that people will not see us, but they will only see the glory of the Bridegroom whom we re-present. I believe we see a powerful picture of this in Revelation 19:

> *And the angel said to me, "Write this: 'Blessed are those who are invited to the marriage supper of the Lamb.' " And he said to me, "These are the true words of God." 10 Then I fell down at his feet to worship him, but he said to me, "You must not do that! I am a fellow servant with you and your brothers who hold to the testimony of Jesus.*

Worship God. For the testimony of Jesus is the spirit of prophecy."

Revelation 19:9-10

In the context of the revelatory experience of John, the angel is narrating the vision of Babylon the harlot being judged as the people of God are being called to come out of her (Revelation 18). This sets the stage for the marriage supper of the Lamb in Revelation 19. In the midst of the bride, or now the wife, making herself ready, John fell down and worshipped this angel. This is the same John who walked with Jesus for three and half years, saw Him in His resurrected body for 40 days, and also encountered Christ in His glory at the beginning of this visionary experience when he fell as a dead man (Revelation 1:17). What was it about this angel that would cause John to worship Him, knowing that as a seasoned apostle it is forbidden to worship angels? The response of the angel, I believe, is key. He says "Do not worship me; worship God. For I am a fellow servant with you and your brothers who carry the testimony of Jesus!"

Scholars differ on the reason John falls down to worship before an angel, especially because it happens twice (Revelations 19:9; 22:8). We have enough information within the context of Chapter 19 that it would seem reasonable to think that the message was manifesting through the angel as a witness to the degree that John seemed to mistake him for the Messiah. The message in Revelation 19 was, "the bride has made herself ready and it was time for the wedding banquet." Could it be that the messenger looked so much like Jesus that John mistook him for Jesus? To carry the testimony of Jesus Christ is when they only see Him and not ourselves! Paul declares, as mentioned previously, that just as God was in Christ, so ambassadors too stand in Christ's place, as God makes

His appeal through us, declaring, "Be reconciled back to God" (2 Corinthians 5:19). The testimony of Jesus Christ is the Spirit of Prophecy and there is a mature bridal company arising that will learn to walk in such union with Jesus to the point that their lives will prophesy and testify of the very life of Jesus. The bride will be a witness of His resurrection, as she becomes so lost in Him that His life becomes her life. Union with Christ means that as we walk with Him, we begin to grab hold of the truth that apart from Him we have no life. For in Adam all have died, yet in Christ all have been made alive (1 Corinthians 15:22).

> *If then you have been raised with Christ, seek the things that are above, where Christ is, seated at the right hand of God. 2 Set your minds on things that are above, not on things that are on earth 3 For you have died, and your life is hidden with Christ in God. 4 When Christ who is your life appears, you also will appear with him in glory.*
>
> Colossians 3:1-3

Chapter 10
From Servants to Sons:
Advancing the Kingdom

12 So then, brothers, we are debtors, not to the flesh, to live according to the flesh. 13 For if you live according to the flesh you will die, but if by the Spirit you put to death the deeds of the body, you will live. 14 For all who are led by the Spirit of God are sons of God.

Romans 8:12-14

The life of Enoch, as well as the ministry of Jesus leading His disciples, is all about walking into a place of maturity and commissioning in order to fulfill the heart of the Father. Paul declares that the mark of mature sons is when it is the Spirit and not the flesh that leads them. In Romans 8, this thought begins by talking about the power of walking in the Spirit:

There is therefore now no condemnation for those who are in Christ Jesus. 2 For the law of the Spirit of life has set you free in Christ Jesus from the law of sin and death. 3 For God has done what the law, weakened by the flesh, could not do. By sending his own Son in the likeness of sinful flesh and for sin he condemned sin in the flesh, 4 in order that the righteous requirement of the law might be fulfilled in us, who walk not according to the flesh but according to the Spirit.

Romans 8:1-4

Paul states that those led by the Spirit are sons of God and they walk in the Spirit fulfilling the righteous requirement of the law. To live a righteous life is

95

required of the law and the condemnation of the law of sin and death is broken in Christ Jesus. The Complete Jewish Bible translates verse one as, "There is no condemnation awaiting those who are in union with Messiah." There is a strong correlation between *walking in the Spirit* and *the Spirit of Life in Christ Jesus.* It is through our union with Messiah that we truly experience what it means to be free from the law of sin and death. So walking with God also correlates with walking in the Spirit and being in union with Christ. The journey of the Christian walk is to learn through discipleship what it means to be a son who has inherited the kingdom. What does it mean to walk in the Spirit and are there any practical applications? According to Paul, those who walk according to the flesh are supremely devoted to fulfilling the lusts of the flesh and those who are walking in the Spirit live under the influence of Christ. The fruit and actions of our lives are great indicators regarding whether we are controlled by the flesh—the ability to fulfill our own desires, or controlled by the Spirit—the Father's desire to see the kingdom on earth. This is why those who are led by the Spirit are sons of God—they understand inheritance and their heart is to fulfill the will of The Father.

Walking in the Spirit of Life in Christ Jesus

John G. Lake a powerful missionary and healing evangelist in the early 1900's spoke often in his writing about walking in the Spirit of Life in Christ Jesus. During the bubonic plague outbreak in Africa, he had this incredible testimony:

"During that great plague that I mentioned, they sent government ship with supplies and a corps of doctors. One of the doctors sent for me, and said, "What have you been using to protect yourself? Our corps has this preventative and that, which we use as protection, but we concluded that if a man could stay on the ground as you have and keep ministering to the sick and burying the dead, you must have a secret. What is it?"

I answered, "Brother that is the 'law of the Spirit of life in Christ Jesus.' I believe that just as long as I keep my soul in contact with the living god so that His Spirit is flowing into my soul and body, that no germ will ever attach itself to me, for the Spirit of God will kill it." He asked, "Don't you think that you had better use our preventative?" I replied, "No, but doctor I think that you would like to experiment with me. If you will go over to one of these dead people and take the foam that comes out of their lungs after death, then put it under the microscope you will see masses of living germs. You will find they are alive until a reasonable time after a man is dead. You can fill my hand with them and I will keep it under the microscope and instead of these germs remaining alive, they will die instantly." They tried it and found it was true. They questioned, "What is that?" I replied, "That is 'the law of the Spirit of life in Christ Jesus.' When a man's spirit and a man's body are filled with the blessed presence of God, it oozes out of the pores of your flesh and kills the germs[26]."

This quote is not to establish doctrine, but to share the testimony of a man who clearly walked with

---

[26] John G. Lake. "Dominion Over Demons, Diseases, & Death". 2011 Edited by Gordon Lindsay. Christ For The Nations.

God. This is not doctrine or grounds to establish that every believer who grabs hold of the truth of this text will be able to put the plagues in their hands and watch it die! It is interesting though that when asked how this occurs that Lake refers to this Scripture. I believe in principle there is a place in God we are destined to go where disease and sickness has to bow. The journey of the Christian walk is to learn that through discipleship want it means to be a son who has inherited the kingdom. What does it mean to walk in the Spirit and are there any practical applications? According to Paul, those who walk after the flesh are supremely devoted to fulfilling the lust of the flesh and those who are walk in the Spirit live under the influence of Christ. The fruit and actions of our life are great indicators to whether we are controlled by the flesh (the ability to fulfill our own desires), or controlled by the Spirit (The Father's desire to see the kingdom on earth). Those led by the Spirit are sons of God because they understand inheritance and their heart is to fulfill the will of The Father. What does it mean to walk in the Spirit? Is it a mystical statement that is meant to not be understood and how does it affect our daily lifestyle?

For the law of the Spirit of life has set you free in Christ Jesus from the law of sin and death.

Romans 8:2

Those who are in union with Christ Jesus walk and abide with Him daily, therefore discipleship directly correlates to abiding in Christ daily. He is the Vine and we are the branches that through discipleship we produce the fruit of His nature (John 15:1-5). Walking in union with Christ sets us free from the law of that produces death. Paul declares that in Adam all died, but in Christ all are made alive (1 Corinthians 15:22). Just as the branch partakes of the life of the Vine and cannot live apart from it, we cannot live with continually walking and abiding in Him.

John the Apostle writes that the law came through Moses, but grace and truth came through Jesus (John 1:17). The law was a shadow point to the reality that found in Jesus. Moses prophesied that a Prophet like him would rise from among them and you shall listen (Deuteronomy 18:15). Just as Moses stood on the Mount and gave the commandments of God to the people, Jesus comes and sits on a Mount and give the commandments of God to His people in the famous "Sermon on the Mount" (Matthew 5:1). Jesus declares the characteristic of the New Testament believer is statements such as "Blessed are the pure in heart for they shall see God" (Matthew 5:8). He also makes a profound statement that will help understand the importance of abiding and walking in the Spirit when He tells them "I did not come to abolish the law and prophets, but to fulfill them (Matthew 5:17). The Greek word for fulfill is "pleroo" which means "to make replete, furnish, to full up, supply liberally, consummate, to carry into effect, bring into realization. To cause God's will (as made known by the law) to be obeyed as it should be, and God's promises (given through the prophets) to receive fulfillment[27]. Essentially, Jesus did not to do away with The Law or The Prophets but He came to bring fulfillment of the prophetic scriptures and cause the law of God to be obeyed as it should. One of the major challenges of Jesus day was the traditions of the Pharisees and Rabbis. "The classical Rabbinic tradition (legal,

---

[27]

https://www.blueletterbible.org/lang/lexicon/lexicon.cfm?Strongs=H5428&t=KJV

discursive, and exegetical) claims to be the Oral Torah, transmitted by word of mouth in an unbroken chain deriving its authority ultimately from divine revelation to Moses at Sinai"[28]. The Rabbis believed the Oral Torah was believed was the interpretation given to Moses alongside the Torah (Law) then passed down to Joshua, the elders and finally the rabbis in succession. There were so many additional commandments added to help keep the law that it began to bring a marred interpretation God's original intent. That is why John the Baptist had to come to prepare the way of the Lord. The traditions were causing the Messiah to be unrecognizable.

After John the Baptist, Jesus arrives on the scene and begins to challenge their interpretations in His Sermon on the Mount when He says:

> [27] "You have heard that it was said, 'You shall not commit adultery.' [28] But I say to you
> that everyone who looks at a woman with lustful intent has already committed adultery with her in his heart.

Matthew 5:27-28

As Moses brought Israel of out Egypt and received the commandments of God to help govern Israel as a kingdom of priests whose king was Yahweh, Jesus the King of kings who came to bring humanity out of a spiritual Egypt also received commandments to

---

[28] Jaffee, Martin S. and Oxford University Press. *Torah in the Mouth: Writing and Oral Tradition in Palestinian Judaism, 200 BCE - 400 CE*. New York: Oxford University Press, 2001. doi:10.1093/0195140672.001.0001

help govern His people. Moses brought the commandments written upon stone; Jesus brought the commandments written upon the heart (Jeremiah 31:33). The law that came though Moses says "Though shall not commit adultery, but Jesus takes it further and declares, "I say even if you lust after a woman in your heart you have already committed adultery with her in your heart"! The commandments that came through Moses dealt with actions, but Jesus brings a revelation of the motives of the heart and transformation. God has always been concerned about the heart, but because of sin, the heart was wicked. Jesus came to establish the law written upon the hearts to bring transform in thoughts and deeds. The New Testament was the Law of Grace and Truth given to govern His ekklesia. That is why the root word to kingdom is walk because in walking with the King, we learn kingdom culture and how to conduct ourselves as inheritors.

Abiding and walking with Christ means, we are walking with The Living Word. Walking with the Living Word does not release information, but transformation and life. In it in Christ that the intent of the commandments of God are revealed and transform us into His image. In discipleship, we are learning the ways of the kingdom and are pruned in the process so that we can produce the fruit of the kingdom. As we learning and grow from walking and abiding in Christ, we are liberated and set free from being governed by the flesh as we learned to be governed by the Spirit. To be a son is to understand that we are embodied spirits who governed by the dictates of kingdom. Sons know that their life in hid in Christ and in Him they live, move, and have their being.

The Blueprint of the Son: It is Time to Build

In Hebrew culture, the son was the builder of the family name and therefore was the reason why the Hebrew words *ben* 'son' and *banah* 'build' "" are closely related. Sons carry the name of their father and with it continue to build the house. Servants do not carry the inheritance of the house, only sons do. For example, the promise of God to Abraham to be a father of many nations had to come through a son and not a servant (Genesis 15:2). Who better to model and show us how to be a son of God than the Son of God who is the firstborn of many brethren (Romans 8:29)?

As Moses entered into the cloud of glory on Mount Sinai, he was receiving the pattern of how to build a sanctuary for God where he would dwell among His people:

> *40 And see that you make them after the pattern for them, which is being shown you on the mountain.*

Exodus 25:40

God told Moses to build according to what you see in the realm of My glory! The word 'build' is *banah* and the word 'pattern' is *tabniyth,* which means *construction, figure, pattern, image, similitude or model.* The root of *tabniyith* is the same two-letter sequence that makes up the word *ben* 'son.' The prophetic pattern Moses was building from was the Son. The blueprint from which discipleship flows is the pattern and image of Jesus who is the perfect and complete expression of sonship. As the disciples walked with Jesus, they were learning from the ultimate blueprint of the kingdom from the King Himself. So complete was the pattern of Jesus the Son that He declared, "-When you see me, you see the Father" (John 14:9).

Learning the lifestyle of the Son comes through walking in intimacy with Him. By doing that we move from being servants who do not know what their master is doing to being sons who walk in inheritance. Growing in maturity will transition us into becoming friends with God who share a common interest and He invites us into co-laboring with Him (John 15:15). Mature sons will only do what they see their Father do, because they will walk in an open heaven (John 5:19-20). The limits will be removed from mature sons, not because they are perfect, but because they have learned the secret of obedience and sacrifice. Jesus, as a son, learned obedience through His suffering (Hebrews 5:8). Jesus, the Apostle, modeled what it means to be a Son who fully re-presents the Father. So likewise, his sons would fully re-present the Son. Our inheritance as sons is to build upon the legacy of the father and to extend the kingdom as joint-heirs with Christ (Romans 8:17).

The Ascension Gifts of the Son: Equipped for Maturity

11 And he gave the apostles, the prophets, the evangelists, the shepherds and teachers, 12 to equip the saints for the work of ministry, for building up the body of Christ, 13 until we all attain to the unity of the faith and of the knowledge of the Son of God, to mature manhood, to the measure of the stature of the fullness of Christ, 14 so that we may no longer be children, tossed to and fro by the waves and carried about by every wind of doctrine, by human cunning, by craftiness in deceitful

103

schemes. 15 Rather, speaking the truth in love,
we are to grow up in every way into him who
is the head, into Christ.

Ephesians 4:11-15

Creation is groaning and waiting for the unveiling of the sons of God (Romans 8:19-22), but only through discipleship can mature sons be released to extend the rule of the King. Reformation within the function of the apostle, prophet, evangelist, pastor, and teacher will be essential to equip the Body to walk worthy of her calling (Ephesians 4:1). The Greek word *doma* 'gift' is important to understand when it comes to the gifts of Christ. *Doma* differs from *charisma,* which is used of the gifts of the Spirit in 1 Corinthians 12. *Doma* "lends greater stress to the concrete character of the "gift".[29] *Doma* is akin to *demo*, which means, "to build"....[30]

Therefore, *doma* of Christ, the Son apostle, prophet, evangelist, pastor, and teacher IS the gift. In the beginning of Ephesians 4, Paul admonishes the Ephesians that in light of the abundance of great and glorious truths that have been revealed to walk worthy of this heavenly calling. It is also a call to walk in unity, as well, which leads right into the grace contained within the *doma* of Christ to help us accomplish it. The purpose of the nature of Christ,--the Son, the Apostle, Prophet, Evangelist, Shepherd, and Teacher—being set in the body is so she can be equipped to grow up into the Headship of Christ and to walk in the full measure of sonship. Walking worthy also means walking in unity with the faith that was once delivered to the saints. It is through discipleship of the *doma* of the Son

---

[29]

https://www.blueletterbible.org/lang/lexicon/lexicon.cfm?Strongs=G1390&t=KJV
[30] Ibid.

of God that we can be *demo* or built up in Him to be sons. It is mature sons who are the legislative body and *ekklesia* that extends the judicial and governmental authority of the Headship of Christ in order to advance the kingdom of heaven on earth.

Advancing the Kingdom

*Now these are the nations that the Lord left, to
test Israel by them—that is, all in Israel who had
not experienced all the wars in Canaan. 2 It was
only in order that the generations of the people of
Israel might know war, to teach war to those who
had not known it before. 3 These are the
nations: the five lords of the Philistines and all
the Canaanites and the Sidonians and the Hivites
who lived on Mount Lebanon, from Mount Baal-
hermon as far as Lebo-hamath. 4 They were
for the testing of Israel, to know whether Israel
would obey the commandments of the Lord,
which he commanded their fathers by the hand of
Moses.*

Judges 3:1-4

The nations that were left in Israel were used by
God to test those in Israel who had not experienced all
the wars in Canaan. The purpose was to teach war to
those who had not known it before. Similarly, every
word that is given to us will be tested as we walk in
discipleship. The Hebrew word *lamad* 'teach' means,
"To be taught, trained and learn". The root of *lamad*
means, "To goad an ox in the right direction, to lead a
disciple or scholar." Just as there were enemies in the
land of Israel that needed to be removed, there are
enemies within our "land" that also need to be removed.
The Angel of the Lord caused Israel to confront the
enemy occupants in the land of Israel and drive them
out (Exodus 23). The revelation of the kingdom will
cause us to confront every occupant in us that stands in
opposition to our assignment. Walking with God is
confrontational because He will make you deal with
your stuff. The Caananites and all the inhabitants of the
land had to be driven out completely, and the Angel or

messenger would go before them. We can see a pattern throughout Scripture of repentance and preparation for divine assignment that comes through warfare. This warfare is not one that happens outside of us, but it is the war within as we walk with God. He goads us to confront what hinders us from producing the fruit desired and fulfilling our assignment. To advance the kingdom within us, Holy Spirit will bring us to every area in our life that needs to be transformed and matured in order to be true ambassadors of the kingdom. The authority must advance within us first, so that we carry the authority with us to see it manifest outside of us as we operate as ambassadors.

Driving Out the Occupants

Years ago, The Lord was bringing me through what I referred to as a "school of the Spirit" regarding angelic activity, as well as the correlation between angels and the word. During this time, my wife and I were meeting with a family who attended the church we were pastoring in order to facilitate reconciliation. At the end of the meeting, we all held hands to seal what the Lord did in all the family members, but as we stood there, suddenly, angels appeared behind all eight family members. I asked the Lord what was happening and He said to me, "The angels are messengers that carry a message for each family member. Whatever is in them that will hinder the fulfillment of the covenant they made, that message will drive it out". When I shared with the family what the Lord said, suddenly and simultaneously the entire family began to be delivered radically, for about an hour! The angels showed us the obstacles and drove out occupants as they took up residence. It was one of the most incredible and unusual deliverance sessions I ever seen. Later as I sought the

Lord for clarity, He revealed to me this type of deliverance we will see more of in the days to come. As we are walking out the message of the revelation of Jesus within, it will cause us to confront every place the enemy is taking residence and will hand out eviction notices. We are moving away from just casting out demons and leaving the house empty, but instead we are walking through the process of deliverance and evicting demons while Christ takes up full residence in us.

The Lord will have a mature body of people who are not afraid to confront the enemy within, so they can remove the hooks the enemy can use to hinder God's people from fulfilling God's assignment. Peter was sifted as wheat in order to test the word in his heart and Jesus declared, "When you are converted, go and strengthen your brothers" (Luke 22:31-32). May the Father have an *ekklesia* who testifies just as Jesus did when He said, "The prince of this world is coming and he has nothing in me" (John 14:30).

The Spirit of Adoption and Inheritance

15 For you did not receive the spirit of slavery to fall back into fear, but you have received the Spirit of adoption as sons, by whom we cry, "Abba! Father!" 16 The Spirit himself bears witness with our spirit that we are children of God, 17 and if children, then heirs—heirs of God and fellow heirs with Christ, provided we suffer with him in order that we may also be glorified with him.

Romans 8:15-17

The goal of discipleship as we walk with God is to be conformed to the mature of image of Christ. It is in the revelation of sonship that we will understand how to walk in divine inheritance. One of the most profound truths regarding sons and inheritance is the Spirit of Adoption. Charles Spurgeon explains the Spirit of Adoption this way:

> "While **adoption** is not the way we get into God's family, it is the way we come to fully enjoy God's family. Adoption gives us the rights of children. Regeneration gives us the nature of children: we are partakers of both of these, for we are sons.[31]"

The Greek word for adoption is *huiothesia*, from *huios*, 'a son' and *thesis* 'a placing.' We are born by the Spirit into the family of God through regeneration (John 3:3-5). *Huios* is the word for a son where *teknon* is the word for child or children. Thus, adoption is about the positioning of sons to walk in their inheritance, not the placing of believers into God's family. According to Vines, *adoption* is a term involving the dignity and relationship of the believer as a son.[32] According to Paul, he groaned for the full adoption which is the redemption of the body (Romans 8:23). Walking with God is the journey from childhood to maturity, which is no different than that of going from a servant to the place of a mature son. This is why Paul tells the Galatians that a child is no different from a servant, though he be lord of all (Galatians 4:1). The sons of a family were given tutors and governors until the father deemed they were mature enough to walk in the responsibility of their inheritance according to the

---

[31] https://www.preceptaustin.org/adoption

[32] https://www.blueletterbible.org/lang/lexicon/lexicon.cfm?Strongs=G1390&t=KJV

father's will or testament. The *oikonomos* 'governor' is the same word translated 'steward' in 1 Corinthians 4:1:

> *This is how one should regard us, as servants of Christ and stewards of the mysteries of God.*

1 Corinthians 4:1

Oikonomos were fiscal agents, house distributers, and overseers over the house distributing hidden treasures to bring the body to maturity. *Okionomos* comes from *okios* 'house' and *nomos* 'law.' Stewards and governors are parceling out the revelation of the gospel of the kingdom to bring sons to maturity so they can walk in the responsibility of the kingdom.

Jesus, who is our blueprint, presents a powerful picture for us when at the age of maturity for Jewish families (30 years old) He was baptized, the heavens opened over Him, the Holy Spirit descended like a dove, and the Father declared, "This is my beloved *huios* in whom I am well pleased" (Matthew 3:17). The Father was now working through the Son to reconcile the world to Himself and it is the desire of the Father to bring many sons to maturity and to reconcile the world to himself through Christ in them by the word and ministry of reconciliation.

Chapter 11
Conclusion

Walking with God in discipleship has been an incredible journey for me over the last twenty years. The ancient path of discipleship is being restored as the hearts of the fathers and the children are being turned toward each other.

> 5 *"Behold, I will send you Elijah the prophet before the great and awesome day of the Lord comes6 And he will turn the hearts of fathers to their children and the hearts of children to their fathers, lest I come and strike the land with a decree of utter destruction.*

Malachi 4:5-6

Discipleship is part of the family that is concerned about passing on inheritance. Discipleship happens within a community that lives according to kingdom culture. The Spirit and power of Elijah comes to prepare the way to walk in kingdom culture. The coming reformation must begin with the restoration of authentic discipleship. Just as Enoch was yoked to Elohim learning to walk in His ways, we are invited to walk in His ways as we prepare for the coming reformation.

In conclusion, one of the most important threads to the restoration of discipleship is intimacy. It is in the place of fellowship with Jesus we will learn the heart of the Father. The heart of the Father is revealed as we walk in the council of the Lord and received His counsel. Intimacy is where we learn to know Him and the power of His resurrection as well as the fellowship of His suffering (Philippians 3:10). The *ekklesia* will arise out of intimate fellowship with Jesus in a community immersed in the kingdom culture. The King has a family of inheritors that He is eager to see them walk in their inheritance. All of creation is groaning and waiting for the unveiling of the sons of God and it through discipleship these sons will mature to walk out their responsibility of inheritance.

Bibliography

Ancient Hebrew Lexicon Bible. https://www.biblestudytools.com/lexicons/hebrew/

Abigail Brenner M.D. 2015. "5 Benefits of Stepping Out of Your Comfort Zone". Psychology Today.

Albert Barnes Commentary on The Whole Book of Matthew. Retrieved from: https://www.studylight.org/commentaries/bnb/matthew.html

Barnes, Albert (1962). *Barnes' Notes on the New Testament* (Complete and unabridged in one volume). *Grand Rapids, Michigan*: Kregel Publications. *ISBN 9780825493713*

Jeff Benner. Ancient Hebrew Research Center. Retrieved from: http://www.ancient-hebrew.org/vocabulary_definitions_god.html

Gerig, W. L. (1996). Walk. In Evangelical dictionary of Biblical Theology (electronic ed., p. 806). Grand Rapids: Baker Book House.

Heiser, Michael S. *The Unseen Realm: Recovering the Supernatural Worldview of the Bible.* Bellingham, Washington: Lexham Press, 2015.

Neudecker, Reinhard. "Master-Disciple/Disciple-Master Relationship in Rabbinic Judaism and in the

Gospels." *Gregorianum* 80, no. 2 (1999): 245-61.
http://www.jstor.org/stable/23580264

Made in the USA
Coppell, TX
26 March 2021